The Fire of
Divine Love

The Fire of Divine Love

Readings from

Jean-Pierre de Caussade

Edited and introduced by

ROBERT LLEWELYN

TRIUMPH™ BOOKS
Liguori, Missouri

Published by Triumph™ Books 1995
Liguori, Missouri 63057-9999
An Imprint of Liguori Publications

First published in Great Britain 1995
by Burns & Oates,
Wellwood, North Farm Road,
Tunbridge Wells, Kent TN2 3DR

Library of Congress Cataloging-in-Publication Data

Caussade, Jean Pierre de, d. 1751.
    [Lettres spirituelles. English]
    The fire of divine love : readings from Jean-Pierre de Caussade / edited and introduced by Robert Llewelyn.
      p. cm.
    ISBN 0-89243-827-4 (alk. paper)
    1. Spiritual life—Catholic Church. 2. Love—Religious aspects— Catholic Church. 3. Catholic Church—Doctrines. 4. Caussade, Jean Pierre de, d. 1751—Correspondence. 5. Jesuits—France— Correspondence. I. Llewelyn, Robert, 1909- . II. Title.
BX2349.C37813 1995
248.4'82—dc20   95-16616

Selections are from *Self-abandonment to Divine Providence: Abandonment to Divine Providence* by Jean-Pierre de Caussade, translation © 1987 by Algar Thorold, TAN Books & Publishers, Inc., and are used by permission.

9 8 7 6 5 4 3 2
First printing
Printed in Finland by Werner Söderström Oy

Contents

Caussade:
The Man and His Teaching

It is one of the great disappointments awaiting a lover of Caussade's writings that not more is known of the man himself. Beyond the names of the places in which he worked, and the various offices which he held, we know almost nothing. In vain did I once visit (in 1971) the lovely cathedral city of Albi, knowing it had twice been the centre of his work.[1] I had hoped to learn more of one who had been my constant companion for more than thirty years and whom I now dared to count as a friend. However, to my disappointment and surprise, no one whom I met, and they included cathedral clergy and convent Sisters, had any knowledge of him, and this although he had been at one time spiritual director and at another time rector of the Jesuit seminary in that place. There certainly appears to have been no Caussade cult and it is only in relatively recent years that he has become widely known. There is good historical reason for this. Caussade lived in a world which was still being shaken by the conflict between Bossuet and Fénelon over Madame Guyon and the Quietist heresy, and there can be little doubt that it was feared that the early publication of his letters might invite an examination of his own orthodoxy. In common with many writers on the deeper aspects of the spiritual life, and, indeed, probably more so than most, Caussade scattered here and there sentences and illustrations which, uprooted from their context, and examined in isolation from contrary considerations to be found elsewhere, would have laid him open to the charge of sharing the heresy he is often at pains to refute. He uses several times, for example, an illustration whereby one sees oneself as a statue in the making, passive in the hands of the Master Sculptor, hammered and chiselled and chipped at the Master's will for the completion and perfection of the work. It might be said that there are strong Quietist overtones here. Yet no one in his senses would suggest that Caussade meant the example to be pressed beyond reason, and he does in fact inject into his illustra-

---

1. See page 53.

tions some such phrases as 'passive acceptance,' or 'obedient response' or 'patient waiting' which would be meaningless in relation to an inanimate object. It will be clear to any comprehensive reader of Caussade that there is a balance in his writing that places his orthodoxy beyond doubt.

Life and Writings

Although Caussade wrote one book,[1] it is in the reading of his letters—spontaneous, deeply discerning and full of warmth and vitality—that the picture of the man irresistibly presents itself. Father James Joyce, S.J., writes:

> The style is the man, and from the style of the letters we get a picture of a man of delightful spontaneity, of verve and vigour, but tender, sympathetic and humorous. He is subtle but logical, humble but sure, straight, forceful and firm yet gently persuasive and always encouraging and patient. Obviously Caussade was a man of fine character and charm and of high spiritual attainments and spiritual gifts. No wonder his treatise and letters have become one of the favourites among spiritual classics.[2]

Caussade was born in Toulouse in 1675, in which year, if we may place him in historical perspective, Fénelon would have been twenty-four, Bossuet forty-eight, and Madame Guyon twenty-seven. His two main teachers, St Francis de Sales and St John of the Cross, had been dead fifty-three and eighty-four years respectively. He entered the Jesuit novitiate when he was eighteen and at thirty was ordained to the priesthood: he died in 1751 at the age of seventy-six. The various places in which he ministered need not detain us here, but we may note that it was while he was at Nancy in 1731—his

1. The treatise on Abandonment is not here classified as a book by Caussade, it being rather an edited collection of his conferences and letters, as will be clear later.
2. Quoted from 'A Biographical Note' by James Joyce, S.J., included in *Self-Abandonment to Divine Providence* (Burns & Oates, 1955).

second sojourn in that town—that he became spiritual director to some of the Visitation Sisters living there. Almost all his published letters are addressed to these Convent Sisters, being written during the period 1730-42, when Caussade was between the ages of fifty-five and sixty-seven. Many letters, it is true, are not dated, but if it be correct that none was written after 1742 this may have been due to his increasing blindness, one of the few personal facts of his life that we know. Of this affliction Father Joyce writes that Caussade bore it with courageous fortitude and in the spirit of his own great principle of abandonment to the will of God.

Caussade's book, to which I have referred, though no doubt valuable to students as an exposition of the prayer life, is written in a dry and catechetical style and was prompted partly (one supposes) by his desire to clarify his position in relation to the Quietist heresy. Although its English translation is published under the simple title *On Prayer*, it originally bore the wearisome inscription, 'Spiritual instructions of the various states of prayer according to the doctrine of Bossuet, Bishop of Meaux,' and was published anonymously as from 'a Father of the Society of Jesus.' Caussade's treatise on Self-Abandonment to Divine Providence was not, as we have seen, originally written as a book, but owes its origin to notes of conferences and letters to the Visitation Sisters, collected and arranged by Mother Thérèse de Rosen, who was herself a recipient of many of the letters. This manuscript was circulated semi-privately after its completion in 1741. About a hundred years after Caussade's death the writings came into the hands of a deeply spiritual Jesuit priest, Paul Ramière, who edited and published them in France in 1860 under the title *L'Abandon à la providence divine*.[1]

---

1. English readers today know Ramière's compilation mainly through two translations, one by E. J. Strickland (Catholic Records Press, Exeter, 1921) and the other by Algar Thorold (Burns & Oates, London, 1955), though the treatise translated by Algar Thorold has also been published by Collins as a Fount paperback.

The Meaning of Abandonment

'Abandonment to divine Providence' is probably the phrase most people associate with Caussade. What, we may ask, did he mean by it? We have already noted that the illustration of the statue in the making, passive in the hands of the Master, gives less than the complete picture. A further illustration, I suggest, may be found in considering how we learn to float. What is it that we must do? We shall at once say that we must abandon ourselves to the water, trusting it, welcoming it, giving it every opportunity to do its work. We shall know that as soon as we begin to struggle—it may be through anxiety, or doubt or fear—everything will be lost and the water will engulf us. At first sight we might think that this example is not far removed from that of the statue, for floating has all the appearance of a passive experience. It would, however, be more accurate to call it a passive activity, for elements both active and passive are present in the process. The one who floats has throughout the operation to be making almost unseen and unperceived adjustments to correspond with the action of the ripples or waves. These movements have their counterpart in the spiritual life in the almost unrealized, imperceptible acts of faith, hope and love made in correspondence to God's action upon the soul.

The complementary nature of these two illustrations will be at once apparent, the one of the statue giving life to the agent but not to the recipient, whilst in the other the roles are in large measure reversed. Taken together they do, I think, give a very fair picture of what Caussade means by abandonment to the divine Providence.

The above illustrations may be helpful but they are not to be seen as exhaustive. If they remain unbalanced by other thoughts, they could take us perilously near to the Quietism against which we have warned. It is not so much that they are inadequate as that they might all too easily be misunderstood. For the man or woman deeply immersed in the life of the Spirit, they are a safe guide, and they may, too, provide at times a valuable corrective for activists whose tendency is to be frequently one or two steps ahead of the Holy Spirit. Particularly they are well suited to the many circumstances which in their outward manifestation we may do little or nothing to change. They may be found especially applicable for most of us in situations calling for acceptance and offering, or, as we sometimes call it, passive response. These two words are, of course, far from being synonymous with 'doing nothing.' On the contrary, such occasions call for the mobilization of all the energies of the soul for the disinfection or transfiguration of the evil encountered. It was no part of Christ's mission to come down from the cross; it was through patient offering and endurance that the victory was won.

Life, however, has many facets and if we were to call on either of our illustrations, let us say to get us out of bed on a cold morning, it is safe to speculate that most of us would be late for work. Many everyday situations such as the one we have posed - the settling down to some uncongenial piece of work, the saying of an Office when we would prefer to read the newspaper, the visiting or helping of some person in need—call for an energetic assertion of the will in the direction of some form of outward action; and although God may be seen as the prime mover in all that we do—'Prevent [Go before] us, O Lord, in all our doings ...,' as the familiar collect has it—neither our floating nor our statue illustration will fit readily into situations such as these. It will be better here if we consider a related theme in Caussade's writing, faithfulness to the duty of the present moment. Abbot John Chapman, regarding Caussade's insistence here as his special contribution to ascetic literature, expressed this in a startling phrase, "The Sacrament of the Present Moment." [1]

---

1. Introduction to *On Prayer* by Abbot John Chapman, OSB (Burns & Oates, 1964), p.xix.

The Sacrament of the Present Moment

Every moment, Caussade is at pains to remind us, has its unique and special part to play in the unfolding of God's purpose. It may be that it brings with it the impress of God's grace inviting us to some task we had neither planned nor foreseen, and the freedom and flexibility to attend to what the Spirit reveals will be a mark of every surrendered Christian life. But, and here, too, Caussade would have us carefully attend, God's will is equally manifested and fulfilled through our faithful and prompt attention to the obligations of our state.[1] The first calls for a sensitive and gentle yielding to the pressure of God's action, the second for a generous and wholehearted commitment to the duty to be done. Abandonment to divine Providence has to be protected from the semi-quietism leading to a state of near inertia scarcely distinguishable from sloth. Caussade is alive to the dangers inherent in abandonment by those who falsely see it as an easy option to an ordered and disciplined life. It is salutary to bear in mind that his treatise and letters are directed toward Sisters who are, indeed, to learn to yield to the special and varied operations of God's grace, but this from the structured background of community life, which no less represents the manifestation of God's will. The important thing is that at whichever level the response to God is to be found, it is made from within the context of the complete surrender of the self, or, in Caussade's more familiar words, abandonment to divine Providence.

The Divine Providence

We have spoken of abandonment: what are we to say of the nature of the divine Providence to whom it is to be made? In two clear and direct sentences Caussade summarizes his teaching as follows:

> Remember our two great principles: 1. That there is nothing so small or so apparently indifferent which God does not

---

1. See especially Treatise, Book 1, chap. 1, section 8.

ordain or permit, even to the fall of a leaf. 2. That God is sufficiently wise, and good and powerful and merciful to turn even the most, apparently, disastrous events to the advantage and profit of those who humbly adore and accept his will in all that he permits.[1]

Everything, then, is to be seen as coming ultimately from God's hands. If we cannot see a circumstance as being directly sent, then at least we are to receive it as part of God's permissive will. Moreover, there is nothing that may not be turned to good account if we will, by God's grace, but remain faithful and responsive in the situation which meets us.

Caussade vividly illustrates his point in the treatise by asking us to reflect that the fish which leapt out of the water to devour Tobias became the food and medicine on which the next period of his life was sustained.[2] That our trials may become the strong point through which God may mediate his grace is a principle ever present and vibrant in Caussade's writings. 'Most gladly will I glory in my weakness that the power of Christ may rest upon me' is a text that takes us to the very heart of his teaching.[3]

Faith, Hope and Love

But how is it that we are to be sustained in times of trial and distress when events press heavily upon us and darkness threatens to overwhelm us? At such times we cannot understand God's action, nor hear his voice, and, most difficult of all, our feelings may be numbed and dry. It is faith, says Caussade, in all its bareness and nakedness, that is to be our support, and some of his most eloquent writings are reserved for this theme. Faith, it has been said, is continuing with what in our calmest moments we know to be right, even when mood and emotion

---

1. See page 38.
2. Treatise, Book 2, chap. 4, section 9.
3. 2 Corinthians 12:9.

are carrying out a blitz on our reason.[1] Caussade would be in full accord, and in almost ecstatic terms he writes:

> The life of faith is nothing less than the continued pursuit of God through all that disguises, disfigures, destroys and, so to speak, annihilates him ... faithful souls endure a constant succession of trials. God hides beneath veils of darkness and illusive appearances which make His will difficult to recognize; but in spite of every obstacle these souls follow Him and love Him even to the death of the Cross.[2]

It is not, however, in the special events, but in the little everyday actions that our faith will be chiefly revealed. Caussade reminds us how for the most part Mary and Joseph lived very ordinary lives. Mary does and suffers what others in her situation do and suffer. She visits her cousin Elizabeth as other relations do; she lodges in a stable in consequence of her poverty; she lives quietly with Jesus and Joseph who work for their living.[3] It all looks so very like what happens to many others. Wherein, then, lies the difference? It is in the faith that discerns every moment as lying within the providence of God. Faithful souls, Caussade tells us, must see God in everything for 'there is not a moment in which God does not present Himself under the cover of some pain to be endured, of some consolation to be enjoyed, or of some duty to be performed.'[4] Were we but more vigilant we would say in every happening, 'It is the Lord' and accept every circumstance as a gift from God.[5]

But, further, it was Caussade's teaching that wherever faith was present, hope and love were active too. Abandonment, he tells us, is a mixture of faith, hope and love in one single act, uniting the soul to God and his action. We have here a trinity of mystical virtues and this state of abandonment can with

---

1. C.S. Lewis, *Mere Christianity* (Fontana, 1952), Book 3, chap. 11.
2. Treatise, Book 1, chap. 2, section 2.
3. Treatise, Book 1, chap. 1, section 2.
4. Treatise, Book 1, chap. 2, section 1.
5. *Ibid.*

equal justification be designated as pure faith, pure hope and pure love. As perfect faith does not lack love, so perfect love lacks neither abandonment nor faith. In times of obscurity and darkness the soul may apprehend its state as one of faith; in times of light and blessing it will appear as love. Yet rather than talk of perfect faith or love, Caussade prefers to speak of the complete abandonment of the soul to God's action, making it clear that all will obtain the special state God has prepared for them. Our call in Christ is simply that our good intention may be united to him so that he may guide, direct and befriend us accordingly.[1]

A Further Image of Abandonment

Caussade supplies us with another powerful picture of abandonment under the image of a plunge.[2] We may picture to ourselves the bathers at the seaside who run headlong down the beach and with complete abandon throw themselves into the waters; and, by contrast, others (ourselves perhaps!) who test the temperature first with their toes and work slowly up and up until at last they are submerged. The twofold picture has its obvious counterpart in the spiritual life and it is clear where generous souls will stand. Caussade's own picture, however, is not of a plunge into the waters—a relatively friendly element—but into the 'deep abyss' of God's will. The idea of generous and wholehearted surrender is still present but the abyss suggests cavernous depths threatening our destruction. We may believe that the image has been chosen with care, for this plunge into God's will may often have about it all the appearance of loss and deprivation; and it is only the eye of faith that enables the soul to discern that in reality the plunge is not into death, but rather—through a measure of death to the superficial self—into a deeper and fuller life. It is not without significance that the picture is provided in the context

---

1. For the whole para, see Treatise, Book 2, chap. 1, section 3.
2. Treatise, Book 1, chap. 2, section 3.

of one of Caussade's most passionate descriptions of the life of faith. Here in this image of the plunge into the abyss we have preserved for us the generous, wholehearted, spontaneous and care-free nature of abandonment, and at the same time the teaching that our deepest good is often shrouded in darkness, which faith alone can discern as the herald, not of death, but of a new richness of life.

The Fire of Divine Love

Our book takes its title from the reading on page 77. We are to consider a piece of green wood thrown on the fire to be acted upon by the flames. It will not catch light at once but will sizzle and twist and sweat until the flames can lay hold upon it and consume it. In some such way the fire of divine love acts upon the raw material of our human nature, as yet full of imperfections and self-love. Purification and refinement and clearance of the dross there must be, and this cannot be achieved without stripping and wounding. But the time will surely come when the flame will lay hold upon the wood; even so will the divine action seize upon the soul, making it as one with the living fire.[1]

Robert Llewelyn

---

1. The illustration occurs several times in the writings of St John of the Cross and it may be that Caussade first met it there. Compare especially with the stanza beginning: 'O living flame of love/That tenderly wounds my soul/In its deepest centre....' St John of the Cross, *The Living Flame of Love*.

The quotations from Caussade throughout this Introduction are taken from E. J. Strickland's translation. See page 125.

The Fire of Divine Love

The providential ordering of life

To avoid the anxieties which may be caused by either regret for the past or fear for the future, here in a few words is the rule to follow: the past must be left to God's measureless mercy, the future to his loving providence; and the present must be given wholly to his love through our fidelity to his grace.

When God in his goodness sends you any difficulty, such as those troubles which used to cause you so much pain, you must first of all thank God for them as for a great grace that is all the more useful for the great work of your perfection, the more it upsets the work of the present moment.

Strive, in spite of your interior repugnance, to be pleasant to importunate people or to those who come to inform you of these troublesome visitors; you must at once leave your prayer, reading, choir, Office and everything in order to go where Providence calls you; and you must do what is asked of you tranquilly, peacefully, without hastiness or vexation.

When you fail in one of these matters you must immediately make an act of interior humility, but not of that irritated, resentful humility of which St Francis has so much to say; it must be a gentle, peaceful and unruffled humility.

Let us understand clearly that we shall not acquire true conformity to the will of God until we are perfectly resolved to serve him according to his will and pleasure, and not according to our own. In all things seek God alone and you will find him everywhere, but more so in those things in which you most of all renounce your own will.

Counsel on prayer

On the subject of prayer I have only two things to say.

Begin it with an entire acquiescence in God's good pleasure, whether this be for your success or to try you with the cross of dryness, distractions and helplessness.

But if you find it easy and full of consolation, then give thanks to God for this without attributing it to your own efforts or dwelling on the pleasure you gain from it yourself.

If your prayer does not go well, submit yourself to God, humble yourself and go away contented and in peace even when there may have been some fault on your part, redoubling your trust and self-abandonment to his most holy will.

With these two points in mind, persevere, and sooner or later God will give you the grace to pray as you ought.

But never, never be discouraged, however helpless and unhappy you may feel.

On saying the Office

As for divine Office, here are three easy and very sound methods.

The first is to keep yourself in the presence of God, reciting the Office in a spirit of great recollection and union with God and raising your heart to him from time to time. Those who are able to recite it in this way must not trouble themselves about any other method.

The second method is to concentrate on the words, keeping yourself united with the spirit of the Church, praying when it prays, sorrowing where it sorrows, and gathering instruction from what is instructive for us; praising, adoring, thanking, in accordance with the different meanings of the verses you are saying.

The third method is to reflect with humility: I am at this moment united with saintly souls praising God, but how I lack their holy dispositions! You must prostrate yourself in spirit at their feet saying to yourself that they are so very much more intent upon God, more full of piety and fervour than ourselves. These sentiments are very pleasing to his divine Majesty and we cannot impress them on our mind and heart too deeply.

Interior direction

We attain to God through the annihilation of self. Let us keep ourselves down so low that we disappear from our own sight.

The more we banish from ourselves all that is not God, the more we shall be filled with God. The greatest good that we can do to our souls in this life is to fill them with God.

The practice of perfect self-annihilation consists in having no other care but to die wholly to self in order to make room for God to live and work in us.

To surrender ourselves to God by a total abandonment of self, and to lose ourselves in the abyss of our nothingness so as to find ourselves again only in God, is to perform the most excellent act of which we are capable, and which contains in itself the substance of all the other virtues. This is the one thing necessary which our Lord recommends in his Gospel.

To lose oneself in one's nothingness is the surest means of finding oneself again in God. Let us practise then a simple remembrance of God, a profound forgetfulness of ourselves, and a humble and loving acquiescence in God's will. By this single practice we shall avoid all evil, and we shall make all things useful for us, and pleasing to God.

We must not distinguish between rest and work, either interior or exterior: it is all one when we keep ourselves in complete acquiescence and interior repose. It is good to note this.

How to deal with excessive fears

We must bear with humility before God the shame of our faults. After committing acts of unfaithfulness to grace or falling by surprise into some fault, we must retire into our nothingness, in a holy contempt of ourselves. This is the great benefit which God makes us draw even from our faults.

When fears for any fault we have committed become excessive, they obviously come from the devil. Instead of giving way to this dangerous illusion, we must repel it with the utmost steadfastness, letting these anxieties drop away from us, like a stone falling to the bottom of the sea, and never entertaining them voluntarily. If however by God's permission these feelings are stronger than our will, we must have recourse to the second remedy, which consists in letting ourselves be crucified unresistingly, since God permits it, just as the martyrs used to do, yielding themselves up to their executioners.

What we have just said about fears which accompany more definite faults applies equally to the feeling of disquiet and distress which arises from the frequency of small infidelities. This heaviness of heart comes likewise from the devil. We must therefore spurn and fight it like a real temptation.

Yet sometimes with certain souls God makes use of this anguish and excessive dread to try them, to purify them and to make them die to themselves. When we cannot succeed in driving them from the mind, no other remedy remains but to bear this crucifixion peacefully in a spirit of total self-abandonment to the will of God. This is the way to restore peace and calm in a soul that is truly resigned to God's will.

Right intention in saying the Office

Fears concerning the recitation of the divine Office are nothing but a pure temptation since actual attention is not necessary.

For prayer to acquire its full merit it is sufficient for it to be made with virtual intention, which is nothing but the sincere intention of praying well which you have at the beginning and which you do not detract by any voluntary distraction.

Thus you can say your Office very well while at the same time patiently suffering continual and involuntary distractions. The distress caused by these distractions arises evidently from nothing but the desire to pray well, and so it is the best proof that this desire is still present at the bottom of your heart.

Now this desire is a good and true prayer; though hidden from the soul by the disturbance which the distractions cause, it is there none the less, and it is none the less perceived by God who gives us a double grace: firstly in hearing our prayer as he hears every prayer that is made well, and secondly by concealing this from us so as to mortify us everywhere and in everything.

Temptations and inner sufferings

Violent temptations are in God's view great graces for a soul. They are an interior martyrdom. They are those great struggles and great victories which have made great saints.

The acute distress and cruel torment suffered by a soul when attacked by temptations are the sure sign that it never consents, at least with that full, entire, known and deliberate consent which makes a mortal sin.

During the violence and darkness of frequent temptations, it is very possible for a tired and troubled soul to commit small faults through frailty, negligence, surprise or weakness; but I maintain that in spite of these little faults it merits more, and it is more pleasing to God and fundamentally better disposed for the reception of the sacraments than the common run of people who being favoured with feelings of sensible devotion have almost no struggle to endure, and have to do almost no violence to themselves. The virtue of the first is much more solid for having endured and for still enduring severer trials.

The majority of people who are not very far advanced in the ways of God and the interior life esteem only the operations of sweet and sensible grace. But it is certain that the most humiliating, distressing and crucifying workings of grace are the most effective in purifying the soul and in uniting it intimately with God. And so the masters of the spiritual life agree in saying that we make greater progress by suffering than by action.

The intention in prayer

Inability to think or make acts during prayer must not sadden your soul. The best part of prayer, and indeed its essence is the wish to do it. Before God, desire counts for everything, in both good and evil.

Now this desire amounts to anxiety in a soul such as yours; it is merely too intense, and it needs only to be restrained. Let the soul maintain itself in peace at prayer, and come away from prayer likewise in peace.

As for direction of intention, the soul abandoned to God should not make too many acts, nor consider itself obliged to express them in words.

The best thing for it would be to rest content with feeling and knowing that it is acting for God's sake in simplicity of heart. Good interior acts are those which the heart makes itself, as by its own momentum, almost without thinking about them.

The great principle of the spiritual life is to do everything, both interiorly and exteriorly, in peace, gently and smoothly, as St Francis de Sales recommends so often. From the first moment of wishing to make an act it is already made, because God sees all our desires, even to the preparation of our hearts.

As Bossuet says, 'Our desires are in God's sight what the voice is for men, and a cry that is held back in the depths of the soul is worth a cry uttered to heaven.' Moreover, all acts made in aridity are very good, and are normally better and more meritorious than acts which are accompanied by feelings of devotion.

The virtue of self-abandonment

You do well to devote yourself vigorously and, as it were, uniquely to the excellent practice of a complete self-abandonment to the will of God. Therein lies for you the whole of perfection; it is the easiest road and leads soonest and more surely to a deep and unalterable peace; it is also a sure guarantee of the preservation of that peace in the depth of our soul through the most furious tempests.

The soul that truly abandons itself to God has nothing to fear from the most violent storms. Far from doing it any hurt they will infallibly serve not only to increase its merits, but also to establish it more and more firmly in that union of its own will with the divine will which renders the tranquillity of the soul invariable.

What happiness, what grace, what confidence for the next life, and what unalterable peace for the present one is to be found in having our being in God only, in possessing nothing more than God alone, no other support, no other help, no other hope!

What a beautiful letter one of your sisters has just written me on this point! For a month, she says, she has had but one thought: God only; I have nothing left but God, and that thought alone consoled, sustained and encouraged her so powerfully that, instead of regrets, she felt within her a deep peace and inexplicable joy. It seemed to her that God took the place of director and friend and that he wished himself to be everything to her.

The more deeply these sentiments penetrate us, the more solid will be our peace; for the decision definitely taken to seek nothing but God and to will only what he wills is above all else that *goodwill* to which the reward of peace has been promised.

The nature of pure love

It is true that even the purest love does not exclude from the soul the desire of its salvation and perfection, but it is equally incontestable that the nearer a soul approaches to perfect purity of love the more it turns its thoughts away from itself in order to fix them on the infinite goodness of God.

The divine goodness does not oblige us to repudiate the reward that it destines for us, but it has surely the right to be loved for itself without any backward glances at our own interests.

Such a love which does not exclude, but is independent of, the love of ourselves is what all theologians call pure love, and they all agree that the soul is more perfect in proportion as it habitually governs itself by the motive of that love, stripping itself entirely of all self-seeking, except in so far as its own interests are subordinated to those of God.

Moreover, total self-abandonment, without reserves or limits, has no thoughts for its own personal interests: it thinks only of God, his good pleasure, his will, his glory; it knows and it desires to know nothing else.

God arranges everything for our good

When I have done what I think before God I ought to do, the success of that enterprise will be what he chooses. I abandon that question entirely to him and with my whole heart, thanking him for everything in advance, desiring only in everything and everywhere his holy will, because I am convinced by faith and by many personal experiences that everything comes from God, and that he is powerful enough and a good enough Father to bring all issues to the best advantage of his dear children.

Did he not prove that he loved us better than his life when he laid it down for love of us? And can we not be assured that having done so much for us he will not forget us? I beg of you, do not distress yourself about me or what I am doing.

Do what I strive to do myself. As soon as I have taken a decision before God and according to his will, I leave all the care of it to him and entrust him with its success. I expect success with confidence, but also with calm and I am willing for it to occur, not in accordance with my own impatient desires, but at the time of divine Providence, which regulates and arranges everything for our greater good, although we usually understand nothing of what it is doing. How can we judge it, poor ignorant creatures that we are, as blind moles living underground?

Let us accept everything from the hand of our good Father, and he will keep us in peace in the midst of the greatest disasters of this world, the fashion of which passes away in a flash. Our life will be holy and tranquil in proportion as we trust in God and abandon ourselves to him. Without that self-abandonment there is no solid virtue, no sure repose.

Freedom in the midst of cares of office

I am touched by your sympathy in my trials, but I am glad to be able to reassure you.

It is true that at first I suffered acutely on seeing myself burdened with a quantity of business and anxieties contrary to my liking for solitude and silence, but see how divine Providence has come to my aid. God gives me the grace to remain unattached to all these affairs, so that my spirit remains always free. I leave their successful issues to his paternal care so that nothing distresses me.

Often things go all right and I give thanks to God; sometimes everything goes wrong. I again bless his holy name and offer him the sacrifice of my efforts. Once this sacrifice has been made, God arranges everything. Already our good Master has prepared several of these surprises for me.

As for leisure, I have more than anywhere else. At the moment visits are rare because I only pay them out of duty and necessity. Our Fathers themselves, who know my tastes, soon finish their business with me and, as they are convinced that I do not act as I do out of pride or misanthropy, no one disapproves of my behaviour and several are edified by it.

Moreover, I am not as dead as you think; but God gives me the grace not to bother about disapproval when I am following the path on which he calls me. Our concern is to please him only; if he is content, that is enough for us, all the rest is a mere nothing. In a few days we shall make our appearance before this great God, this sovereign Master, this infinite Being. Of what use then (and for all eternity) will anything be that was not done for his sake and animated by his grace and Spirit?

It is necessary to help ourselves

How can we doubt that God understands our interests much better than we do and that his dispositions of events in regard to us are advantageous even when we do not understand them? Would not a little wisdom be enough to determine us to allow ourselves to be led with docility by his Providence, though we cannot understand all the secret springs which God brings into play, or the particular ends he has in mind?

But, you will say, if it is enough to let us be passively guided, what becomes of the proverb: 'Help yourself and God will help you'? I do not say that we must not act: no doubt we must help ourselves; to fold our arms and expect everything from heaven, whether in the order of nature or that of grace would be an absurd and sinful quietism. But while we are cooperating with God we must never cease to follow his direction and lean upon him.

To act is this way is to act with assurance and consequently with calm. When one looks upon oneself in all one's actions as the instrument of divine Providence and aims at nothing but fulfilling God's designs, one acts gently, without trouble or hurry, without disquiet about the future or regret for the past, abandoning oneself to God's fatherly Providence and counting on it more than all possible human means.

In that way, one is always at peace, and God unfailingly directs everything for our good, either temporal or eternal, and sometimes for both.

A joyful discovery

I have discovered something here which gives me more satisfaction than all imaginable delights. There is in this town of Albi a convent of Poor Clares totally cut off from the world who enter religion without any dowry and live on alms from day to day. The superior is one of the holiest persons I have known in my life. I felt at once a great interior attraction to be in holy relations with them and most of them have admitted that they had the same attraction toward me. I believe that God is preparing some great graces for me by means of their prayers. They are very interior souls and practice self-abandonment to God in great perfection.

When I said to them that on every occasion that offers, I would endeavour to procure alms for them, they seemed to me almost scandalized and begged me to think only of making them more spiritual, more detached and more holy by my instruction and by my prayers. Nothing can be imagined more admirable than their sisterly union, their candour and their simplicity.

Struck by their great austerities, I asked them one day whether the hardship of their life did not greatly damage their health, and shorten their days: they replied that they hardly ever had invalids among them, and that very few died young, and that most of them lived till past eighty. They added that their austerities and fasts contributed to fortify their health and to prolong their lives, which a too plentiful regime would shorten.

Never have I seen more gaiety and joy than among these saintly women. This is indeed an occasion to praise and bless God for his wonders in the souls of his servants.

Trusting God in all things

I do not understand your anxieties, my dear Sister; why do you insist in tormenting yourself over the future, when your faith teaches you that the future is in the hands of a Father who is infinitely good, who loves you more than you love yourself and who understands your interests far better than you? Have you forgotten that everything that happens is directed by the orders of divine Providence? But if we know this how can we hesitate to remain in a state of humble submission to all that God wishes or permits?

How blind are we when we desire anything other than what God wishes. He alone knows the dangers which threaten us in the future and the help which we shall need. I am firmly convinced that we should all be lost if God gave us our desires, and that is why, as Augustine says, God, in his mercy and compassion for our blindness, does not always grant our prayers, and sometimes gives us the contrary of what we ask as being in reality better for us. How many troubles and useless anxieties injurious to our peace of heart and spiritual advancement would not this one principle, rightly understood, dispel! Shall I never succeed with the help of grace in instilling into your mind and still more into your heart this great principle of faith, so sweet, so consoling, so loving and so pacifying?

When one is illuminated by heavenly light, one thinks very differently from most men, but what a source of peace, what power one finds in this way of thinking and looking at things! Let us study to give all our care and intention to the task of conforming ourselves in all things to the holy will of God in spite of interior revolt. That revolt in itself must be accepted in obedience to the will of God, which permits it in order to accustom us to remain at all times and in all circumstances before him in a state of sacrifice and with a self-abandonment full of confidence.

God's providence is over all

Remember our great principles:

1. That there is nothing so small or apparently trifling, even the fall of a leaf, that is not ordained or permitted by God.

2. That God is sufficiently wise, good, powerful and merciful to turn the most seemingly disastrous events to the good and profit of those who are capable of adoring and humbly accepting all these manifestations of his divine and adorable will.

Let us be perfectly persuaded that God arranges everything for the best. Our fears, our fussiness and our tendency to worry often make us imagine trials where there are none. Let us follow the leading of divine Providence one step at a time; as soon as we see what is asked of us, we also will desire it and nothing further. God knows far better than we, poor blind creatures that we are, what is good for us.

Our pains and troubles often come from the granting of our wishes. Let us leave everything to God, and all will go well. Let us abandon everything to him *in toto*; that is the only way to provide surely and infallibly for our true interests; I say: our *true* interests, for we have also false interests leading to our ruin.

My self-abandonment to divine Providence, as I conceive and recommend it, is not so heroic or so difficult as you think. It is the centre of the solid peace of the soul and there only is found the unchangeable repose which the most trying events cannot ruffle.

God's action in the depths of the soul

The mainspring of the whole spiritual life is goodwill, that is the sincere desire to be God's, fully and without reserve: you cannot, therefore, renew this holy desire too frequently in order to strengthen it and make it constant and efficacious in you.

The best way to drive off useless thoughts is not to combat them openly and still less to allow oneself to be troubled and disquieted by them, but just to let them drop, like a stone into the sea; little by little the habit of letting them drop makes this salutary practice quite easy.

The second way of thinking of nothing but God consists in a sort of general forgetfulness of everything, at which one arrives through the habit of letting drop our useless thoughts, so that, for some time, one may pass whole days without thinking, as it seems, of anything at all, as if one had become stupid.

Often, indeed, God places certain souls in this state, which is called emptiness of the spirit and of the intelligence; it is also called being in nothingness.

The annihilation of our own spirit disposes us wonderfully to receive that of Jesus Christ. This mystical death of our own activity renders our soul apt for the reception of divine operations.

The purgation of the will

This great emptiness of spirit of which I have spoken some-times produces another emptiness which is more painful, namely emptiness of the will, so that one seems to have no feeling at all for the things of the world or even for God, being equally insensible to everything.

Often indeed it is God who produces this second emptiness in certain souls, so that one should not try to get out of this state which disposes us for the reception of the most precious workings of God in us.

It is a second mystical death which must precede our happy resurrection to an entirely new life. We must esteem and cherish this double void, this double self-annihilation so hard to self-love and the spirit of pride, and accustom ourselves to this state in an interior spirit of holy joy.

Two governing principles

You are quite right in what you say, my dear daughter, and indeed the great maxim of Mother de Chantal was: 'Not so many questions, so much learning and writing, but sound practice.'

As regards souls that have acquired the habit of avoiding deliberate faults and faithfully fulfilling the duties of their state of life, all practical perfection may be reduced to this one principle: the exercise of a continual resignation to the manifestations of the will of God, a complete self-abandonment to all the exterior or interior dispositions of his Providence, whether in the present or in the future.

There is no mystery about the way to reach that point; only two things are necessary. First, the profound conviction that nothing happens in this world, in our souls or outside them, without the design or permission of God; now, we ought to submit ourselves no less to what God permits than to what he directly wills. Second, the firm belief that through the all-powerful and paternal Providence of God, all that he wills or permits invariably turns to the advantage of those who practise this submission to his orders.

Supported by this double assurance, let us remain firm and unshakeable in our adhesion to all that it may please God to ordain with regard to us. Let us acquiesce in advance in a spirit of humility, love and sacrifice in all imaginable dispositions of his Providence; let us protest that we wish to be content with whatever satisfies him.

We shall not always be able, no doubt, to feel this contentment in the lower (the sensitive) part of our soul, but we shall at least preserve it on the heights of our spirit, on the fine point of our will, as St Francis de Sales says, and in those circumstances it will be even more meritorious.

On the means of acquiring self-abandonment

Here, in a few words, is what you ought to do in order to attain promptly to pure love and perfect self-abandonment.

You must, first of all, ardently desire and energetically will it, whatever price you have to pay.

Secondly, you must firmly believe and say repeatedly to God that it is absolutely impossible for you to acquire by your own strength such perfect dispositions, but, also, that grace makes everything easy, that you hope to receive this grace from his mercy, and you must beg it of him in and through Jesus Christ.

Thirdly, you must gently and quietly humble yourself, whenever you have withdrawn yourself from the holy bondage of his will, without discouragement, but on the contrary protesting to God that you will await with confidence the moment at which it will please him to give you that decisive grace that will make you wholly die to yourself and live to him by a new life wholly hidden with Jesus Christ our Lord.

Fourthly, if you are docile to the inspirations of God's spirit, you will take care not to make your advancement depend on the warmth and sensible sweetness of your interior impressions. The divine Spirit will, on the contrary, make you esteem rather his almost imperceptible operations, for the more delicate and profound they are, the more divine they are and so much more removed from the impressions of the senses.

One belongs more totally to God then, because one tends to him and to union with him with all one's powers, and the whole extent of one's being, without particularizing any special point. For every being seeks its centre.

All consists in loving well

Do not distress yourself so much at being so frequently at war with your wretched nature; heaven is worth all these battles. Perhaps they will shortly come to an end and you will achieve a complete victory. After all, they will pass, and rest will be eternal. Be at peace and let your humility always be mingled with confidence.

Try with peaceful fidelity to profit by all the various states through which our Lord may wish you to pass for his glory and your own perfection. Turn all that happens in the direction of divine love and a simple self-abandonment to the paternal guidance of God's adorable Providence. Try, in fine, to become humble and simple like a little child, from love and so as to imitate our Lord in a spirit of peace and recollection. If God finds this humility in us, he will himself cause his work in us to advance. Let us persevere and be faithful to grace for the greater glory of God and for his pure love. Everything depends on truly loving, in heart and deed, the God of goodness.

When God gives us special tastes in devotion, special sensibilities, let us profit by them to attach ourselves more firmly to him beyond all his gifts. But in times of dryness, let us always keep the same attitude, humbly recalling our indulgence, and considering also that perhaps God wishes to prove the solidity of our love for him by these salutary trials.

Let us be truly humble and occupied in the correction of our faults, and we shall not think much about those of other people. Let us see Jesus Christ in all our neighbours, and we shall not find it hard to excuse them, to endure and cherish them. Let us turn our quick temper on to the task of glorifying God in ourselves and in those whose confidence he gives us. For the rest, let us charitably endure ourselves as it is our duty to endure others.

The prayer of divine repose

This is what I should reply with regard to the person in question: her prayer of recollection seems to me to proceed rather from her head than her heart. This is the inverse of what ought to be, for in order that this kind of prayer should bear fruit, it is necessary that the heart should be more applied to it than the intelligence.

It is, in fact, a prayer wholly of love: the heart, reposing sweetly in God, loves him without distinguishing clearly the subject of its love, or how this love is produced in it. The reality of the prayer is clearly shown by a certain ardour which is continually experienced in the heart, by a constant tendency toward the divine centre of our being which continues without any clear intellectual perception, and by the overpowering attraction to which the soul yields without possibility of distraction. From this comes the great facility of this kind of prayer, which is a sweet repose for the heart and which continues without effort almost as long as one wishes.

Let us thoroughly persuade ourselves that God can be found everywhere without effort, because he is always present to those who seek him with their whole heart, though he may not always cause his divine presence to be felt. For instance, when you happen to be entirely unoccupied with created things so that you seem to be thinking of nothing and desiring nothing, you should know that then your soul is unconsciously occupied with God and in God.

Thus, the true presence of God is, to speak exactly, nothing but a sort of forgetfulness of creatures with a secret desire of finding God. It is in this that interior and exterior silence consists, so precious, so desirable and so profitable: the true earthly paradise, where souls who love God enjoy already a foretaste of heavenly joy.

The hiddenness of the Holy Spirit's work

You have only to go on as you are doing, but explain yourself in a way that would distress those without experience of this state of prayer.

You say that you do nothing, and yet you are always doing something or you would be in a state of pure idleness; but your soul acts so gently that you do not perceive your interior acts of consent and adherence to the Holy Spirit.

The stronger these inspirations are, the less you should act; you should merely follow what is drawing you and allow yourself to be drawn gently on, as you rightly say.

Your manner of behaving in times of storm and upset enchants me: submission, total self-abandonment without reserve, being content with lack of contentment when God wills it. In those conditions one advances more in one day than in a hundred filled with sweetness and consolations.

Your total, continual and universal self-abandonment to God through a sentiment of confidence and union with Jesus Christ, always doing the will of his Father, is the most divine and surest method of success in everything; try to communicate it to everyone.

Finally, if there is some little act of reparation to be made to our neighbour, let us never fail in this duty, but take the opportunity to conquer generously our pride and human respect.

The test of solid virtue

If when we are ourselves exposed to various criticisms and unjust prejudice, we persevere in our line of conduct without change, following the guidance of Providence step by step, we are truly living by faith alone, with God alone in the midst of the quarrels and confusions with creatures.

In such a disposition of soul, external things cannot reach our interior life, and the peace which we enjoy can be troubled neither by their favours nor their contempt. This is what is called living the interior life, and a very interior life it is.

Until this independence of soul has been acquired the most apparently brilliant virtues are in reality very fragile, superficial and liable to corruption by self-love, or to be upset by the slightest breath of inconstancy and contradiction.

Be well on your guard against all illusions, which, however specious they may be, incline you to follow your own ideas and prefer yourself before others. A self-sufficient and critical spirit seems to many but a trifle, but we cannot deny that such a spirit is greatly opposed to religious simplicity and that it prevents many souls from entering on the interior life.

For, indeed, we cannot enter the path of that life unless the Holy Spirit, who never gives himself save to the humble-minded and the simple, introduces us to it.

Do not become attached to God's gifts

When, in the course of prayer, you experience certain attractions, such as a sweet repose of soul and heart in God, receive these gifts with humility and thanksgiving, but without becoming attached to them.

If you loved these consolations for their own sake, you would oblige God to deprive you of them, for when he calls us to prayer it is not in order to flatter our self-love and give us an occasion for self-complacency, but to dispose us to do his holy will and to teach us an ever-increasing conformity to that will in all things.

When distractions and dryness follow these consolations, you know how you should endure them: that is, in peace, submission and self-abandonment according to God's good pleasure in permitting them.

You know also that the only harmful distractions are those of the will; it follows that those which displease you do not impede the prayer of the heart and the desire. Never force yourself to fight obstinate distractions; it is a safer and better policy to let them drop, as one lets drop the various absurdities and extravagances that in spite of ourselves pass through our mind or imagination.

What has already happened will often happen again. What God may have refused you during prayer, he will give you when it is over, so as to make you realize that it is the pure effect of his grace and not the fruit of your own labour and industry.

Nothing is more useful for keeping us in a sense of our dependence on grace and of abjection in our own eyes; this is the source of true humility of heart and mind.

The strength of peace to the soul

You should remember all your life that one of the principal causes of the small progress made by certain good people is that the devil continually fills their souls with disquiet, perplexities and troubles, which render them incapable of serious, gentle and constant application to the practice of virtue.

The great principle of the interior life lies in peace of the heart: it must be preserved with such care that the moment it is in danger everything else should be abandoned for its re-establishment.

Peace and tranquillity of spirit alone give the soul great strength to achieve all that God wills, while trouble and disquiet turn the soul into a weak languishing invalid. In that state one feels neither zest nor attraction for virtue, but, contrariwise, disgust and discouragement, by which the devil never fails to profit.

This is why he makes use of all his ruses to rob us of this peace on a thousand specious pretexts: at one time on pretence of examination of conscience or of sorrow for our sins, or at another time on the ground that we are abusing grace and that our total lack of progress is our own fault, in short that God is about to abandon us; and by means of a hundred other dodges against which few are able to defend themselves.

This is why the masters of the spiritual life give this great principle for distinguishing the true inspirations of God from those that come from the devil, namely, that the former are always gentle and peaceful and lead us to confidence and humility while the latter are agitating, unquiet and turbulent, leading to discouragement and suspicion, even to presumption and the following of our own will. We must therefore firmly reject all that does not bear this mark of peace, submission, gentleness and confidence, the impression, as it were, of God's seal: this point is of great importance for the whole of our life.

Let God act

Your present method of prayer comes much more from grace than from yourself. You should, therefore, let grace act, and remain in an attitude of humble docility, calmly and simply keeping your interior gaze fixed on God and your own nothingness. God will then work great things in your soul without your knowing what is happening.

Beware of all curiosity on the subject, be content to know and feel the divine operation; trust yourself to him who is working in you and abandon yourself totally to him, that he may form you and shape you interiorly as he pleases.

Have no other fear in these happy moments but that of attaching yourself rather to his gifts and graces than to the Giver. Do not esteem or savour these graces except in so far as they inflame you with divine love and help you to acquire the solid virtues that please the divine Lover: self-abnegation, humility, patience, gentleness, obedience, charity and the endurance of your neighbour.

Be sure that the devil is not the author of these favours, and that he will never be able to deceive you so long as you make your zest and sweetness serve toward the acquisition of the solid virtues that the Faith and the Gospel teach and prescribe to us.

Let God act; place no obstacle through your natural activity to his holy operation, and be faithful to him in the slightest things.

Living for God alone

The simplest ideas and those that lead to a spirit of holy childhood and filial confidence are always the best in prayer. How agreeable to God and how all-powerful with him are prayers that are at the same time simple, familiar and respectful. How I wish for you the continuation of this simple and humble gift of prayer, which is the great treasure of the spiritual life!

You say that you do not understand how you have passed from dislike of your state to so perfect a love for it. The explanation of this, my dear Sister, is that by various interior operations, your soul has been, so to say, recast as an old tin or silver pot is recast, so as to become new, beautiful and shining. There will be much more recast in your soul, if you are well detached from consolation, faithful to grace and wholly resigned to the good pleasure of God, in aridity, pain and desolation.

I agree with you in thinking that God wishes you little by little to die to everything, to live only to him, for him and by him: to have neither thoughts, desires, designs, pretensions, affections, joys, fears, hopes, nor love save for God alone. But you will have to suffer cruel agonies before arriving at this entire detachment, which is called, and truly is, a mystical death.

But be of good cheer. God will support you, and in order to do so he will give you from time to time a breathing space by foretastes of heaven and delicious sweetness, which he will cast into your soul like a heavenly manna to feed and strengthen it while crossing the desert.

The path of pure faith

Profit by your experience never to abandon on any personal ground the simple way of pure faith, to which God has introduced you.

Do not forget that in this way the operations of God are almost imperceptible. The work of grace is accomplished in the most intimate part of your soul, in the part of the soul's depth that is furthest from the senses and consequently from sensible experience.

To strengthen your steps remember, first, that this way is what Jesus Christ was referring to, when he said we should adore the heavenly Father in spirit and in truth.

Remember, second, that the sensible side of grace is but the dregs, and, thirdly, that the simpler, deeper and more imperceptible the operations of God, the more spiritual, solid, pure and perfect they are.

A peaceful spirit with oneself and others is one of the greatest gifts of God. Follow that spirit and all his inspirations: he will work wonders in your neighbour and yourself.

When one has learnt how to remain in peace in one's soul, God holds his divine school in the soul when he teaches everything without noise of words to attentive, peaceful and docile souls in such a way that directors have nothing to say but: 'Listen attentively to the voice of God's spirit,' or better still: 'Follow faithfully the interior impulse of his grace.'

Advice to a woman of the world

This is what you must do throughout your stay in the country. The obedience you give to my directions will bless this time of rest and ensure you all its benefits.

Go to the sacraments as often as it is thought fit for you to go. Each morning offer up to God with the pleasures of the day the trials both exterior and interior with which it shall please his goodness to season them, and at intervals repeat the words: 'For all things and in all things may God be blessed. Lord, may your holy will be done!'

Now that you are less busied with others, spend more time in nourishing your soul with good reading. To make this nourishment the more beneficial, let this be your method of taking it. Begin by entering the presence of God and by begging his help. Read softly and slowly, a word at a time, that you may interpret your subject with your soul rather than with your intelligence. At the end of each paragraph containing a finished thought, pause to appreciate what you have read or to rest yourself and to gain interior tranquillity before God. When you notice that your attention is wandering, go back to your reading, constantly making similar pauses as you continue. If you find this method useful to your soul, there is nothing to prevent you adopting it during the time set aside for meditation.

Busy yourself during the day with such useful work as obedience has entrusted to you and as is in the plan of divine Providence.

Be at pains to cast out all vain and useless thoughts, as soon as you are aware of them; yet do this peacefully without effort or violence. Cast out in particular all unquiet thoughts, relinquishing to divine Providence everything tending to preoccupy you.

A biographical note

I am back again at Albi with its mild climate and its friendly folk whose only fault from the point of view of a lover of solitude like myself is that they are too friendly. The many invitations which I receive will become a real cross to me while God will doubtless send me others to moderate the delight I take in seeing for the fourth time a countryside I have always greatly loved.

God be blessed for all things! He scatters his crosses on every side; I, however, have made all my sacrifices - have accepted and made offering in advance of all the trials it shall please him to send me.

This attitude adopted well beforehand makes such trials far milder when they materialize and much less considerable than the imagination pictured them. Nevertheless I am delighted to be where God would have me as the direct result of his loving Providence that for ever leads me by the hand. His fatherly care, of which I perceive myself to be the constant subject, still further strengthens my trust.

Though my health is consistently good, I am conscious that the swiftly passing years bring us nearer to that eternity to which we all must come. A few days back one of my friends remarked to me that in growing old like myself he found that time seemed to pass incredibly fast, that weeks appeared to him now as short as days in the past, and months as weeks, and years as months. In point of fact, alas! what do a few years more or a few years less amount to when we are to exist as long as God himself?

Nothing will comfort us so much in death as our humble submission to the various plans of divine Providence, despite the insidious promptings of self-love that so often come under the most spiritual guises and most plausible pretexts.

Lord, have pity upon me

Bear in mind the saying of St Francis de Sales: 'You do not put on perfection as you put on a dress.' In this, the secret you ask of me is to be found in the seeking. Impress it thoroughly upon yourself, that your longing may sink slowly into your self.

Everything good in you originates from God, everything evil, spoilt and corrupt originates in yourself. Set aside then, nothingness and sin, evil habits and inclinations, abysmal weakness and wretchedness. These are your portion. These originate in, and unquestionably belong to, you.

Everything else—the body and its energies, the soul and its senses, the modicum of good you have performed—is God's portion. It so manifestly belongs to him that you realize you cannot claim one whit of it as yours, nor feel one grain of complacency, without being guilty of theft and larceny against God.

At frequent intervals repeat interiorly: 'Lord, have pity upon me; with you all things are possible.' There is nothing better or more simple than this; nothing more is needed to call forth his powerful help. Hold powerfully to these practices and inclinations. God will do the rest without your perceiving it.

I am inwardly convinced that, failing some great unfaithfulness on your part, by his blessed works God will effect many things in you. Regard this as certain; do nothing willingly to obstruct it. Should you perceive that unhappily you have done so, humble yourself without delay; return to God and to your true self, showing always complete trust in divine goodness.

Confidence in God alone

Guard against discouragement, even though you witness the failure of your repeated resolutions to serve God. Your trust in God can never be pushed too far. Infinite goodness and mercy should induce trust as infinite.

If, having asked for grace, you have neither the impulse nor ability to look at the state of your soul, you must remain silent and at peace. Discouragement, so far from being evidence of pure intention, is a dangerous temptation; for progress is to be desired only to give pleasure to God and not to the self.

Your mind, then, is to be content invariably with what God wishes or allows, inasmuch as his will alone must be the standard and the definite boundary of our desires, however holy they be.

Again, the notion that you will reach some particular state must not be entertained, otherwise you will become self-satisfied. The surest sign of our advancement is the conviction of our wretchedness. Then shall we be as rich as we think ourselves poor; our interior humiliation will increase, and with it our distrust of ourselves and our readiness to depend upon God alone.

God has begun to make you this gift. Be not anxious therefore, nor discouraged. Say to yourself: 'Today, I am going to make a start.'

Remedies in sickness of soul

If your intentions are truly good, if you are seriously and energetically resolved to belong to God, you must make every effort to remain in a state of peace that the message of the angels may not be falsified—peace to men of goodwill. You must expect, however, that Satan will make every effort to prevent you from attaining that wished-for peace. I am convinced that unfortunately he has met with only too much success recently.

At present your soul's greatest failing is its perturbation, inquietude and interior agitation. Thanks to God, its ills are not incurable; yet so long as they remain uncured, they can only be as disastrous to you as they have been grievous.

Interior agitation deprives the soul of the ability to listen to and obey the voice of the divine Spirit; to receive the delightful impress of his grace, and to busy itself with pious exercises and exterior duties.

A sick and agitated mind is in the same class as a fever-weakened body that can perform no serious work until healed of its complaint. As there is an analogy between the diseases of both, so, too, there are likenesses between the remedies to be applied.

Physical health can be restored only by a threefold prescription: rest, good food and obedience to the doctor's orders. The like threefold prescription will bring back peace and health to a soul troubled and sick almost to death.

The first remedy

The first requirement for your cure is docility. Above all, base your virtue upon renunciation of your judgement and upon a humble and warm-hearted readiness to accept and perform everything your director deems pleasing to God.

If you are animated by the spirit of obedience, you will never allow yourself to be set back by any thought contrary to the direction you have received. Equally you will take good care to avoid the inclination to examine and question everything.

Yet if, despite yourself, thoughts antagonistic to obedience creep into your mind, you will cast them from you; or, better still, you will condemn them as dangerous temptations.

The second treatment for your spiritual sickness is tranquillity and peace of soul. For the attainment of these you must first and foremost long for them and earnestly petition God for them. Secondly, you must bend all your energies toward their acquisition.

I will now answer the question you will probably put as to how you are to set about this.

The second remedy

In the first place take care never to harbour voluntarily in your heart any thought calculated to grieve, disquiet or dishearten it. From one point of view, such thoughts are more dangerous than impure temptations. Your need, then, is to allow them to pass you by, despising them and letting them fall like a stone into the sea.

You must resist them by concentrating your attention upon contrary reflections, and especially upon aspirations designed to this end. Yet while we are to put energy and generosity into our struggle, mildness, tranquillity and peace are as necessary. For unquiet grieving and vexatious restlessness will make the remedy worse than the disease.

In the second place you are to avoid purely human ardour, eagerness and activity in all your efforts, whether exterior or interior. On the contrary you must make it your habit to walk and talk, to pray and read, softly and slowly, putting no strain upon yourself in anything, even though it be resistance to the most frightful temptations.

Remember that the best repudiation of such temptations is the grief they bring you. As long as your free will feels only horror and detestation for the end that these temptations hold out to the imagination, plainly it will give no consent to them.

Remain in peace in the midst of such temptations no less than in spiritual ordeals.

The third remedy

We come now to the remedy for the weakness evinced by a troubled soul as a result of the fever that afflicts it. For such a soul a strengthening diet is necessary.

Let good books be read and this reading be done in a low voice with frequent pauses, less to bring to it the reflections of the intelligence than to allow the mind to digest what it reads. This apt saying of Fénelon's should not be forgotten: 'Words we read are but the leavings, while the relish we have in them is the juice upon which our soul is fed and fattened.' We need to do with spiritual food what the greedy and the sensual do with *ragouts*, sweetmeats and liqueurs, which they still taste and savour, even after they have swallowed them.

At all times shun the pursuit of consolation through vain talk with fellow human beings. This is one of the essentials for those passing through spiritual ordeals. God, who sends us these for our good, wishes us to endure them without seeking consolations other than his own, and ordains that he himself shall determine the juncture at which these consolations shall be bestowed upon us. Each according to his ability and inclination must devote himself to interior prayer, and this with neither strife nor violence, and keep himself quietly in God's holy presence, turning to him from time to time with some interior act of adoration, repentance, trust and love.

If such an act cannot be performed, be content with the earnest wish to perform it, for, in good as in evil, the desire with God is equivalent to the deed. For, as with the spoken word we talk with, petition and thank our fellows, so in God's case all these are achieved by the mere desires of our hearts. These desires speak to and solicit him far more eloquently than any words or even any interior act, such as we call formal and distinct. A cry retained in the depths of the soul is worth as much as a cry raised to heaven.

The continuation of the same

You must set yourself to pray with gentle sweetness and loving tenderness both at morning meditation and at all times throughout the day. Pray either by a constant turning of your heart to God or by gazing interiorly on his divine presence.

Finally, this good food of the soul consists in willing at all times and in all places what God wills; or, to put it otherwise, to obey every command of divine Providence in every imaginable state of soul, interior or exterior, whether in health, sickness, aridity, distraction, weariness or temptation; in all these things saying with the whole heart: 'Truly, O God, I long for all things, I accept all things, to you I make offering of all things, at least I desire to do so. In this I beg your grace; help me and strengthen me in my weakness.'

In bitter temptation you must cry to him: O God, keep me now from all sin. This holy abjection, and interior humiliation and humbling of my pride I gladly accept as much, and for as long, as pleases you.

The weakest and most troubled soul adopting the methods just outlined cannot fail to make its own once more its lost peace and joy.

The perception of our faults

You appear to lack docility, you say, only because you state honestly your doubts and fears. The trouble is not that, dear Sister, but the fact that you cling too fast to these doubts and fears. You concentrate upon them too much, instead of ignoring them and casting yourself upon God in utter self-abandonment, as I have consistently exhorted you for so long. Only through this holy and happy self-abandonment can you ever enjoy an enduring peace full of perfect trust in God through Jesus Christ.

Yet once again, what have you to fear in this self-surrender especially after so many plain signs of God's great mercy to you? You seek for conscious support in yourself and your works and conscience, as if they provided more assurance and stronger support than God's mercy and Jesus Christ's merits, and, under the assumption that these cannot lead you astray, I pray God to enlighten you and to change your heart at last in this matter so vitally important to you.

To get back to your letter: 'I should be surprised,' you say, 'and disconcerted were you able to disclose to me all you see and feel.' My answer to you is this: A lively perception of our failings and imperfections is the grace which befits that state— a very precious grace.

And the reason? First, because such intimate perception of our wretchedness maintains us in humility; at times it avails to inspire us with a wholesome horror and holy fear of ourselves. And secondly, because this state, outwardly so wretched and so hopeless, makes way for a heroic self-abandonment in the arms of God.

Abandonment to be embraced not feared

When we have reached the lowest depths of our nothingness, we can have no kind of trust in ourselves, nor in any way rely upon our works; for in these are to be found only wretchedness, self-love and corruption.

Such complete distrust and utter scorn of the self is the one source from which originate these delightful consolations of souls wholly surrendered to God—their unalterable peace, their blessed joy and their unshakeable trust in none by God.

Ah, would that you knew the gift of God, the reward and the merit and the power and the peace, the blessed assurance of salvation that are hidden in this abandonment; then would you soon be rid of all your fears and anxieties!

You imagine yourself lost as soon as you think of surrendering yourself, notwithstanding that there is no more certain path to salvation than that which leads through complete and perfect self-abandonment.

I have never met a soul more obdurate that yours in refusing to make this surrender to God. Yet you will have to come to it, if only at death. It is utterly necessary then to abandon yourself to God's great mercy.

Faith in Christ alone

But, you will say, I could believe myself warranted in practising this self-abandonment and ridding myself of my fears only if, living a saintly life, I had performed many good works. You delude yourself, dear Sister.

Such a remark on your part can be prompted only by your unhappy self-love that would completely rely on yourself, whereas your duty is to put your trust in God alone and in the infinite merits of Jesus Christ.

You have never had as firm a wish as you should have to perceive this fundamental truth. You consistently stop to examine your doubts and fears instead of disregarding them in order to cast yourself blindly into God's hands and headlong upon his bosom.

In other words, you wish in every case to be given a firm guarantee to make your self-abandonment easier. Assuredly in this there is no true self-surrender to God arising from utter trust in him alone, but merely an unconfessed desire for the self to be assured before that surrender is made to his infinite goodness. So does a law-breaker act, who before he throws himself upon the king's mercy, requires the pardon to be guaranteed!

Is this a call, then, to depend upon God and to base all your hope upon him? It is for you to draw your own conclusions.

The last and costly step

I am stressing this point strongly, because I have been taught by experience that it is here that souls in your state offer their last resistance to grace and the final leap that may free them from the self—a leap that is as difficult as it is necessary.

I seem to have met with no one who has offered as much resistance as yourself. This arises from an extreme self-love, a great and hidden presumption and a reliance upon yourself that you may never have suspected. For make no mistake about it, as soon as this complete surrender to God is mentioned, you are aware of a certain interior upheaval, a feeling that all is lost or that you have been asked to close your eyes and hurl yourself into a deep pit.

The truth is nothing of the kind; in fact it is the exact opposite. For the greatest certainty of spiritual safety in this life is to be found in this utter self-abandonment which, in the words of Fénelon, consists in being driven to breaking-point of oneself so as to have no hope but in God alone.

Such language may at first sight seem fantastically strong; give it your earnest consideration.

Objections answered

What of the question of my salvation? you ask. Can it be that you still do not know the surest guarantee of that, too, is by dwelling only on God, to place the whole burden of that also upon him?

Yet is it not a duty to commune with and to be watchful over the self? Why yes, upon your entrance to God's service when your need is for detachment from the world, withdrawal from exterior things and correction of bad habits previously formed. But afterwards you are to forget self and think only of God.

In your case your one desire is to remain buried in yourself and in what you imagine to be your spiritual interests. To deprive you of this last wretched recourse to self-love, God ordains that you find in yourself only a hot-bed of doubts and fears, griefs and uncertainties, disquietude and defeat.

Such is God's way of saying to you: Do but forget yourself and you shall find in me peace, tranquillity, interior joy and a firm assurance of your salvation. I and I alone am the God of salvation, you by yourself can effect only your perdition.

You may argue further that in this self-forgetfulness you will not even perceive your faults and imperfections, much less correct them. Error, illusion and ignorance are never so clearly perceived as in the clear sight or presence of God. These are like a sun shining interiorly, that, freeing us from the dread of perpetual self-examination, at a stroke reveals to us all we need to know. Equally it serves to consume gradually, as a fire consumes straw, our every fault and imperfection.

A warning against preoccupation with self

Surrender all things to God and in him you shall find all things more abundantly. So shall you rid yourself once and for all of that wretched retrospection, fear, perturbation and anxiety, to which those calculating souls are condemned who would love God only out of love for themselves and who seek their salvation and perfection less to please God and to glorify him than to serve their own interest and eternal welfare.

Yet, you will say, God ordains that we should yearn for salvation and eternal happiness. Undoubtedly; but that yearning must accord with his desire and decree. Now this is God's decree: God created us only to serve his own glory and to fulfil his own purpose. Yet, since also he is infinitely merciful, he willed that his creature should gain his own ends and his eternal welfare by accomplishing God's will.

Precisely the opposite is true in that unhappy self-love which seeks itself in all that it does: first and foremost we think of our own spiritual and eternal interests; thus preoccupied, we relegate to second place that which has to do with the glory of God.

What are we about when we are for ever preoccupied with ourselves? We might well be saying: I should be lost did I not constantly think of my interior needs and did I not as constantly ask how I stand with you and what is to become of me. These must be my ceaseless preoccupation. I can only think occasionally of those things that tend to your glory and gratification.

In the Holy Scripture the divine Saviour has answered clearly and precisely brides of his who use such language: 'He that loveth his life shall lose it: and he that hateth his life in this world keepeth it to life eternal'.

The interior life's first need

Let me in all sincerity disclose a fear I have on the subject of yourself. In my opinion your too frequent contact with your many relatives and others in the world are a stumbling-block to your advancement. Be careful that in wanting to do good to others you do not harm yourself.

Though, because of my calling, I am more compelled than you to keep these contacts with the world, I must confess that I find it for my soul's good to limit them as much as possible. During my stay here I have paid none but necessary visits; while, so far as I am able, I discourage calls upon myself. I speak of God, salvation and eternity to all those who come to see me, this being a rule prescribed by St Ignatius as one he himself used with consistently happy results. If they appreciate this kind of talk they will profit by it, and their visit will not have been a waste of time. If they do not appreciate it, they will stop calling, or at least call less often, leaving me more time to give to my duties as priest.

Our hope to make some progress in virtue will be in vain as long as our minds are filled with worldly talk and our hearts preoccupied with temporal interests. Recollection is the interior life's first need. I cannot urge you too strongly to limit your contacts and to adopt St Ignatius's method in those you think you should keep.

This rule befits no one better than a nun whose vocation vows her to seclusion. Far from being astonished at it, people will be edified by the faithfulness with which she conforms her behaviour to it. If, on the other hand, she is seen too often in the world, people will be scandalized; while in these vain contacts with men, she will lose every grace that could have been hers through contact with God.

On the way of spiritual reading

I send you *Christian Hope*, the book I promised you. It is a real treasure for you. Yet if you are to get all the good from it I expect, you must not plunge too eagerly into it or let yourself be led away by curiosity as to what comes next. Spend the time upon it allowed to you by the Rules: fix your attention upon what you are reading and do not think upon what follows.

I recommend you strongly to assimilate the enduring and consoling truths set out in this book, not so much by mental reflection as by savouring them. Pause now and then to give these glad truths time to soak more thoroughly into your soul, and to make easier the working of the Holy Spirit who, during these peaceful pauses and silent expectancy, will imprint these heavenly truths more deeply upon your heart.

Do all this without straining your attention or too violently curbing mental speculation. Let your unforced and simple endeavour be to allow them to sink into your heart rather than into your mind. You had far better read little and digest that little. Your soul needs, never more than now, unity and simplicity.

Your reading, then, and your actions should have as their one aim the fostering in you of the spirit of recollection. God will gradually grant you this grace, do you but yearn for it with gentle trust and humble simplicity, showing neither precipitancy nor unquiet anxiety.

Beseech God often to detach you completely from everything, that, in and for Jesus Christ, you may have neither liking nor love for any save him, and that, making your heart wholly his, he shall possess it fully and unreservedly. 'O God, I abandon myself to you; make me to desire none but you.'

The harmfulness of indiscriminate zeal

I order you never to speak of God or any holy thing except in a spirit of meekness and humility, and in a manner at once loving and gracious. In such speech be always restrained and encouraging; never bitter and harsh, since this is likely to chill and rebuff those who hear you. For although your talk be only of what is in the Gospel and the best kind of books, I judge that, in the state in which you are now, that talk can take so clumsy a form that nothing but evil results from it.

Truth consists in relating things exactly. It is distorted immediately it is stated extremely or applied unsuitably. Your peevish mood is like a blackened glass which, unless you make allowance for it, prevents you from seeing things and describing them to others in their true colours.

Be always on your guard against this distressing tendency; cherish thoughts and sentiments that counteract such peevishness; assure yourself and make it your delight to assure others of the infinite goodness of God and the trust we should have in him; let your behaviour give them an example of virtue that is neither stiff nor embarrassing to others; take special care never to make harsh announcements to your sisters. When you can find nothing gentle to say, keep quiet, leaving the burden of such pronouncements to others who will find it easier than you to be rightly strict, avoiding too great leniency and too great severity alike.

At all times severity is as blameable as strictness is laudable: it serves only to antagonize minds instead of convincing them, and to embitter hearts instead of winning them. That true gentleness which has God's approval is as calculated to frustrate evil and forward good, as excessive harshness is to make good difficult and evil obdurate. The one builds; the other destroys.

Advice to a novice joining late in life

At last you find yourself free of ties and of all those engage-
ments with which the world would keep you bound for ever. I
have no doubt that you appreciate the full value of this inesti-
mable grace and that you are bent on a generous performance
of all your duties.

The longer you have waited for this grace, the more grateful
you must be to him who has at last accorded it to you.
Nevertheless in your life you must expect to meet with difficulties unknown to those who enter earlier. Yet humiliation,
renunciation, simplicity, and spiritual childhood will consider-
ably lessen these difficulties and will end with making them
disappear.

Aided by these virtues you will avoid one of pride's insidious
illusions—an illusion the more dangerous in that it is almost
imperceptible—into which many novices fall. To show their
zeal they are for ever trying to do something out of the
common, or to deny themselves the little privileges allowed
them by the charity of their superiors.

In all this, is merely vanity and subtle self-love. Never make
claim, my dear Sister, to do one whit more than the rest.
Accept simply and humbly the little privileges and alleviations
offered to the weak; be glad to be ranked with small children
and treated like them, and avoid making yourself conspicuous
by a show of strength and courage. In this is an exercise of deep
and meritorious humility more pleasing in God's sight than a
life whose great austerity is of your own choice. Any other line
of conduct is so much pride and vanity.

The continuation of the same

To be frank with you, my long experience has taught me that those who have been most devout in the world before they enter on the religious life are usually those who give most trouble to their superiors and mistresses; for in the world these good, devout women acquire various ideas of virtue that they find hard to give up.

Used to the admiration of all about them and, very frequently, to the praise of their directors, they become obsessed with their own thoughts and outlook, never suspecting that the obsession is poles removed from true holiness. Consequently, it is much more difficult to induce them to practise humility and renunciation, and to discipline their ideas and wills than to persuade the young and unformed—or even converted worldlings—to make similar sacrifices.

Unless, however, we become as little children we cannot enter the kingdom of heaven. You who are mature, and have been so devout in the past, are to do all that you are told without a question. You are to do it in a spirit of humility and simplicity, content to see yourself like the weakest and least of them all. You are to look at yourself as precisely the latter, and you are to rejoice at it, or as nearly rejoice as you may.

True interior insight and genuine spirituality will teach and inspire you to this. Yet it must be confessed that there is the greatest difficulty in bringing our so-called truly devout to this frame of mind. The less they, poor blind deluded souls, can humble themselves, the farther they are from true greatness. Let them go to Bethlehem and there behold the God of heaven become a little child, taken up, carried here, carried there, at the caprice of all. By becoming like that little child you will be worthy of entering the kingdom of heaven.

A most dangerous temptation

Just now you are victim of one of the most dangerous temptations that can assail a well-intentioned soul—the temptation of discouragement. I adjure you to offer every resistance in your power.

Trust in God, and be sure he will complete the work he has begun in you.

You vain fears for the future come from the devil. Think only of the present; leave the future to Providence. A well-employed present assures the future.

At all times and in all places strive to cleave and conform to all God's wishes even in the smallest matter; for virtue and perfection consist wholly of this.

Again, God permits our everyday faults only to humiliate us! If you can profit by them and yet remain trusting and in peace, you will be in a better state than you would if you committed no obvious fault and so flattered your self-love greatly, leaving you in grave danger of self-complacency.

Actually you can very easily make use of all your faults to become one degree more humble and to dig still more deeply within yourself the one foundation of all true holiness. Ought we not to admire and bless the infinite goodness of God who can thus derive our greatest good from our very faults? All we need do is to have no love for them, and humble ourselves gently because of them; after each of our falls to pick ourselves up with tireless persistency, and to go to work peacefully to correct them.

Be faithful in this practice and you shall dwell in peace even in the midst of perplexity. May he be blessed for all things and in all things, now and for ever.

We grow into deeper freedom

Can a soul wholly given up to a pursuit of recollection, to a conflict with self and the acceptance of many constraints both interior and exterior—can such a soul be expected to appear playfully gay and pleasantly amusing? Indeed, if any do appear so, I gravely doubt whether any interior change has taken place.

Yet are there not, you ask, those whose intense interior life goes with much exterior graciousness? True, but only after long practice that has in a measure made interior recollection natural to them. At the outset they were as you are, my dear Sister. They have said nothing, but have gone their way, till God has at last brought them to that spiritual state known as the freedom of God's children.

You will reach it just as they, have no doubt about that. A day will come when your recollection will be free and unforced, mild and pleasingly gentle. Then you too will make others approve of and rejoice in you because of the exterior peace which the full love of God and your neighbour makes abundantly manifest in you.

Yet you cannot attain this either quickly or at once. For it comes of virtue assiduously practised and of an interior life which, at the beginning, must needs be somewhat forced and difficult. All this will come naturally at the end, however.

Once you have attained this, you can resume your gaiety of manner and unreservedness, since both will then be changed and made spiritual by the blessed workings of grace, whereas at an earlier stage these would certainly do harm.

Over-eagerness a stumbling block

The inclination God gives you to surrender your soul wholly to him and to live, despite the mind's vagaries and the rebellion of the flesh, a wholly interior life, is a grace whose value I wish God would make known to you as he has made it known to me.

Why, then, in spite of the inclination of all your pious reading, are you able to get no farther than the threshold of the interior life? I see plainly that this is the reason, my dear Sister: you have frustrated this inclination by unrestrained desires, by over-eagerness and human activities which are displeasing to God and obstructive to the gentle workings of grace.

Further, the reason is that in your behaviour is a secret and scarcely perceptible presumption that causes you to put too high a value on your own work and efforts. Without taking much account of it, you acted as if you claimed to do all the work yourself and even to do more than God wished.

You who would have considered worldly ambition a great fault have no scruples in allowing yourself to be led astray by a more insidious ambition and a longing for your own exaltation in the ways of the spirit. Yet be comforted: thanks to the merciful sternness God has shown toward you so far, there is nothing lost. In fact you have gained a great deal. With the tenderness of a loving father, God punishes you for these imperfections and offers you the remedy for your ill in the very punishment he awards you. To chastise you for your unfaithfulness, he makes use of the ordeals he employs for the purification and detachment of those chosen souls whom he calls to pure love and divine union.

Try to understand this fatherly attitude God adopts toward you, keep your trials in perspective; then all your fears will vanish of themselves.

Be content to wait on God's action

At the moment your sole need is self-abandonment. This is what you must do to attain it:

In praying you must be resigned to suffer the grievous torment and crucifixion which is God's pleasure. When distractions, dryness, temptations and aversions assail you, you must say: Divine crosses, I am glad of you! I await you with a submissive heart; cause me such suffering that my self-love may be thereby crucified and obliterated. Thereupon you are to stand before God like a beast of burden weighed down by its load almost to the point of collapse, yet hoping for the help and assistance of the Master.

Cast yourself in spirit before the cross of Jesus Christ, kissing his sacred wounds respectfully and lying humbly at his divine feet. Be content, steadily and resolutely to remain there, your passive expectancy and peaceful silence resembling those of a poor wretch who for hours at a time waits for alms upon the threshold of a great king or a generous rich man. Yet in prayer or whatever else it be, see to it that you do not force yourself to be more recollected than God wills.

Avoid violence, then, in your efforts to extend recollection throughout the day and to shun the distractions that beset you. Be content to know that this state of distraction displeases you and that your longing is for greater recollection, when, and to the extent that—and only to the extent that—it shall be God's pleasure.

Uneasiness, foolish fears and depression

While I find no trace of deliberate sin in your behaviour, I do find a multitude of faults and imperfections which will do you much harm unless you attempt a drastic cure. These include anxieties, vain fears, dejection, weariness and discouragement that are half deliberate, or at least not sufficiently resisted, and that constantly disturb in you that interior peace upon the need for which I have been insisting.

What are you to do to prevent them? First, never cling to them voluntarily; secondly, neither endure nor resist them with violent effort since that merely strengthens them. Allow them to drop as a stone drops into water; think of other things; as St Francis de Sales says, talk to God of other things; take shelter in your refuge—the interior silence of respect and submission, of trust and complete self-abandonment.

How am I to behave, you may ask, if whether in this connection or in others, I commit faults, even voluntary faults? On such occasions you must recollect the counsel of St Francis de Sales: neither be troubled that you are troubled, nor be anxious that you are anxious, nor be disturbed that you are disturbed, but turn naturally to God in sweet and peaceful humility, going so far as to thank him that he has not allowed you to commit still greater faults.

Such sweet and peaceful humility, joined to trust in divine goodness, will calm and pacify you interiorly, and this is your greatest spiritual need at present.

Green wood for the burning

When you throw on the fire a dry piece of wood for kindling, the flames catch it first of all and then burn it gently and quietly. But if the wood is still green, the flames envelop it for a moment merely, then the heat of the fire coming into contact with the moist green inner wood makes it sweat and hiss, moves and twists it noisily this way and that, until as a result the wood is dry and in a fit state to kindle. Then the flames again envelop it, set it alight and silently and effortlessly consume it.

There you have a parable of the action and operation of the divine love upon souls which are yet full of imperfections and self-love's evil inclinations. These must be purged, purified and refined—which cannot be done without causing them vexation and suffering. Liken yourself, then, to that green wood upon which the divine love acts before it is able to kindle and consume it.

Or again, liken yourself to a statue in the hands of a sculptor who shapes and fashions it with hammer and chisel to make it fit to be set in a noble building. Had that stone feeling, and in the course of its suffering cried out to you: 'Sister, what shall I do? I am in such pain!' your answer doubtless would be: 'Nothing, except rest and be still beneath the workman's hand, leaving the work to him. Without him you will remain for ever a senseless and unshaped block of stone.'

Let your own motto be: have patience, and let God do the work. For, when all is said, you can do no other. Yours is merely to say: 'I adore and resign myself; may your will be done.'

We must allow God to work in this way

In prayer there can be a gentle and pleasurable peace. But that peace can be also bitter and barren and even sorrowful. God can effect more in our soul by the latter than by the former—liable as it is to the activities of self-love.

Thus, self-abandonment is necessary in this matter as in all others. Leave him to act; he knows our need better than we.

We have but one thing to fear: that we voluntarily allow ourselves to go astray. To avoid the risk of this we have only to wish exactly what God wills at every hour, at every moment, and in every happening of the day. The surest, swiftest, and, I venture to say, the sole way of perfection lies in that. Everything else is liable to illusion, pride and self-love.

To conclude: gently and without too much effort learn to refrain from those lengthy reasonings with which your mind is busied during prayer, and incline rather to loving aspirations, to simple rest and delight in God.

This, however, need not prevent you from dwelling for a little time on good thoughts when their nature is sweet, simple and peaceful, and when they seem to be spontaneous.

The weaning from the idolatry of self-love

Be not wistful, my dear Sister, for the inclinations and the conscious delights God has given you and has now withdrawn from you. Many imperfections were present in the consolations you experienced in that spiritual state.

It is true that while these consolations were perceptible, they greatly gratified your nature whose desire is to see, recognize and experience them without intermission, yet the nearer this state is to the human, the farther it is from satisfying the needs of divine love. Accordingly God is the quicker to withdraw them from a soul whom he sees to be faithful to grace.

The soul that ordeals have not enlightened and made free allows itself to drift, almost unaware, into new recourses to self. It builds its contentment and peace upon that least dependable of all things—the feelings. If it clings to God, it does so not for himself solely but much more for the consolation it expects of him. It cherishes a futile self-esteem based upon the spiritual riches it believes itself to possess, while only God can save it from falling into something like an idolatry of its imagined excellence.

When as a result of a complete change of your spiritual fortunes you see yourself reduced to nothingness, you find yourself suddenly stripped of vanity, presumption and every scrap of self-esteem, and possessed of humility, trust in God and love for him. Moreover your love is now altogether pure, since self-love's last perceptible prop has been taken from it with the result that it has nothing to cling to or corrupt. Thus I find your present state of poverty of more worth than your former fine experiences which, while they seemed so wholly pure to you, provided only so much secret and delightful food for your self-love.

The importance of the fixing of the heart on God

The fact that your thoughts wander is in your case only one more of God's ordeals, providing an opportunity for suffering and humilation, an exercise in patience and an evidence of merit; while the grief that it occasions you is proof of the desire you have to be ever concerned with God.

Now, God sees this desire and in his sight desires, whether good or bad, are the equivalent of acts. Suffer then, humbly and patiently, all these mental distractions, and take good care not to be worried about them or to investigate anxiously the source from which they come.

Remember that St Teresa said on this subject: 'Let the mill-clapper make what noise it will, so only the mill grinds the corn.' She compares the mind's wandering attention to the mill-clapper and the inclination toward God to the mill which grinds the corn. It is for this fixing of the will on God that we must always long.

What do you imagine takes place in a thoroughly worldly woman's mind while she is listening to a fine sermon? Numerous uplifting reflections pass through her mind and her imagination while her will and her heart are concerned with the object of her passion. She is surely not the holier for this? With you the exact opposite happens. Why then be grieved?

Be at peace, then, in your tranquil self-abandonment to God, nor bother to learn how to translate it into acts. These will be done by the secret and invisible stirrings of your heart that God touches interiorly and moves according to his pleasure.

Holy and profitable idleness

The exhaustion and sense of emptiness you feel in longing to increase and attempting to repeat your interior acts do not surprise me. These come of withstanding God's work and acting alone as if you wished to forestall grace and perform more than God wishes. This is merely human activity.

Be content to withdraw peacefully into your soul, staying there as if in a prison in which it pleases God to keep you captive, and making no further attempts to escape. That holy and profitable idleness spoken of by the saints is thus acquired, and those vast tasks accomplished that need no work for their accomplishment.

It is only self-love that grows weary and despondent in doing nothing, seeing nothing and understanding nothing. Yet let self-love grumble to its heart's content. Its very weariness and despondency will rid us of it in the end. By cutting it short of food we shall make it die of hunger—a death to be desired indeed! With all my heart I long for it in your case as I long for it in mine.

The tree is known by its fruits

One of the commonest experiences known to souls who have not yet had much experience in the interior ways is the fear you have told me of: I refer to the fear of wasting time in the prayer that is a simple dwelling in the presence of God.

Such souls can easily be reassured, and so can you. All you need to do is to remember the divine Master's precept: the tree is known by its fruits. What produces only good effects can be nothing else but good. Now, your own experience tells you that since you have adopted this manner of prayer, you have greatly benefited interiorly. You have, then, but to thank God for the favour he has done you in substituting, as he has, the peaceful action of grace for the feverishness of your human activity.

I wish you were in the habit of estimating your spiritual progress and interior state generally by the one infallible standard of faith and Gospel teaching. When you perceive that your ways, your thought and your behaviour are in harmony with the teaching of the faith and the practices of the saints, you can consider them good and perfectly sound.

It is then impossible to fall into the illusion accompanying judgement based on the self and on impressions received through the senses, questionable as these always are. To regulate your conduct by such impressions is to make a compass of a weathercock that veers with every wind.

To a Sister in spiritual darkness

I realize from what you have told me that you are walking in spiritual darkness. Yet I by no means share the anxiety this state causes you. This way is usual enough in persons of your sex; while there is no doubt that it is the safer in being the less exposed to the vain complacency of self-love or the deception of vanity.

This very darkness, therefore, is one of God's graces; for in this life the best means of going to God is to walk by naked faith which is always obscure. Despite this obscurity, you can understand enough about it and can give details of it to make it sufficiently plain to any moderately experienced director. So much for what I think of your state in general. Now to deal with your difficulties in detail.

You say that you cannot pray. Experience has taught me that every person of goodwill who talks in this fashion can pray better than most, since their prayer is simple and humble and in its simplicity escapes being mere formal thought. This kind of prayer involves dwelling in God's presence with a secret and persistent desire to receive his grace according to our needs. Since God sees all our desires, this is the supreme prayer. For, to quote St Augustine, perpetual desire is perpetual prayer. In prayer let your guide be simplicity. Of this you cannot have too much, for God loves to see us like little children before him.

As for holy communion, your growing hunger for the divine fare and the strength it imparts to you are strong reasons for going to it frequently. Give up your fears, then, taking comfort from the assurance I give you.

Prayer of the heart

Your soul's inclination is very simple and what is simple is best. It turns straight to God, and so you must follow it unfailingly and gently, without effort or eagerness either to keep it or recapture it when your perception of it is gone, otherwise you would be claiming God's gifts as your own.

Distractions and dryness are fairly frequent in this type of prayer. Yet these endured with patience and self-abandonment are themselves excellent prayers. Moreover, though these distractions and aridity be painful, they do not hinder that sustained desire to pray that is found in the depths of the heart. Heartfelt prayer is no other than this.

If you have been using this excellent form of prayer for a whole year, or possibly two, a book will not help you. If, however, these periods of helplessness and aridity last for (say) seven or eight consecutive days, by all means take a book, but read it with frequent pauses.

Again, if you find that such reading further distracts or troubles you interiorly, break it off and seek to remain in God's presence in silent peace, so far as you are able.

You must not be surprised—still less must you be perturbed—if what has moved you in the past moves you no longer: such vicissitudes must be endured interiorly as changes of weather and season are endured exteriorly. Not to expect them is to show a singular lack of experience.

Resolutions are rarely used in this kind of prayer. Yet much more good comes of it than of resolutions made during meditation.

Two kinds of interior peace

There are two kinds of interior peace: the one is sensible, sweet and delightful; while, as it does not depend upon ourselves, it is by no means indispensable. The other is almost unperceived and is to be found in the depths of the heart and the most secret recesses of the soul.

Usually it is dry and savourless and it can be possessed during the greatest tribulations. Intense recollection is necessary before it can be recognized; you might imagine that it was buried at the bottom of an abyss. It is the peace in which God dwells and which he himself calls into being that he may dwell in it as in his own element. There in the depths of our hearts he performs his unperceived and marvellous works. These are recognized only in their effects: thus it is through God's beneficent influence that we find ourselves in a state of steadfastness amid grief, violent upheavals, great difficulties and unforeseen afflictions.

If you discover this bare peace and tranquil sadness in yourself it remains but to thank God for it: no more is necessary for your spiritual advancement. Cherish it as the most precious of gifts. Slowly increasing, it will one day be your most precious delight. Conflict and victory must precede that day.

I congratulate you in having adopted my own favourite saying: God wills it! May God be blessed in all things! What comfort there is in that saying! Let us, my dear daughter, make use of it whenever our delicate spiritual stomachs reveal their weakness and their difficulty in dealing with food not to their liking. By this simple recipe bitterness is changed into sweetness and we find everything good and palatable. Nothing is more calculated to uplift our hearts.

True recollection

True recollection lies in the calm that you enjoy in solitude, and in the tranquillity of a mind and heart that are emptied of all created things and are less and less preoccupied. God deprives you of it at prayer time, because you are then too full of desires and eagerness.

Stay then during prayers just as you are during solitude; I require no more concentration and eagerness from you. Keep perfectly quiet and meditative, relinquishing all desire of created things. Then will you dwell with God, though you neither know, feel, nor understand how this can be.

It is a pure truth to believe that you do nothing for God, and that the little you in fact do is spoilt because your self-love mingles with it. From the time when it is God's pleasure to impart this clear knowledge of himself in combination with the humility which his blessed grace inspires, we expect nothing further from self but everything from him. We rely no more upon our good works but upon God's mercy and upon the infinite merits of Jesus Christ. There you have the true Christian hope which saves our souls.

Every other spiritual state, every other spiritual inclination involves such grave risk to salvation; whereas to hope only in God, to rely only upon God, in and through Jesus Christ, is the hard rock, the firm and lasting foundation that no illusion, self-love or temptation can threaten.

Spiritual progress must be in God's time

I must desire my advancement and perfection only so far as God wishes it and by the means that he wishes. Such a desire can only be calm and peaceful, even when it is full of vehemence and fervour.

But there is another desire for our perfection that springs from pride and an immoderate love of our own excellence. This does not depend upon God: consequently it is restless and for ever agitated.

Our need to surrender our soul to the first of these and our need to put all our energy into defeating the second are equally great.

All desire for our advancement, therefore, however holy it appears, must be curbed the moment eagerness, restlessness or perturbation enters into it. Such results can only come from the devil, since all that comes from God leaves us tranquil interiorly.

Why then, my dear Sister, desire with so anxious a fervour spiritual wisdom, interior awareness and appreciation, facility in recollection and in prayer, and every other gift of God, when it is not his will to give these to you yet?

Is not this to wish to perfect yourself to your own liking and not to his, to follow your own will and not the divine will; to have more regard for your taste than for God's; in a word to wish to serve him at your caprice and not in accordance with his good pleasure?

The need to resist over-eagerness

We are in perfect agreement, dear Sister, since you think with me that your activity and over-eagerness are a fault. Fight against them with all your strength. I ask no more than that.

You say that I would wish to see you altogether perfect and without a fault. That is so, and has always been the object of my zeal for you. Yet I do not count it a crime that you have not reached that perfection. I know that this can only come by slow degrees, through great trust in God and great fidelity to his grace. He alone can finish the work in you that he has begun; your own duty is to abandon yourself wholly to him and leave him to do his work.

I am delighted that you feel God upholds you visibly in your difficulties. Live so, in as much peace as is possible and in a great interior silence.

But you tell me that it seems to you impossible to acquire this interior life with your character and temperament. That is so, but what is impossible to man is easy to God. It is upon him alone and upon his grace that you must rely, through Jesus Christ.

To put a kind of compulsion on you to make humility your foundation stone, the God of goodness begins by making you more keenly aware of your weakness. Yet when this feeling casts you down, at once let hope pick you up; for, as you know, it pleases God to turn our greatest weaknesses into triumphs for his grace.

Let your hope be in God

The words that you say interiorly time after time—Lord, who are able to do all things, have compassion on me—make the best and simplest prayer that you can offer. No more is needed to secure his powerful help. Make this your steadfast practice.

Maintain your attitude of expecting nothing of yourself and of putting all your hope in God. He will do the rest without your being aware of it, while I am sure that eventually I shall notice perceptible signs of it. I am interiorly convinced that, short of some great infidelity on your part, God will by his blessed work accomplish many things in you.

Rely implicitly upon that, trying merely to put no voluntary impediment in God's path. When, unfortunately, you know that you have impeded him, humiliate yourself immediately, and return to God and your true self with a complete trust in the divine goodness.

We have only to cleave to God and his holy will by acquiescing in all his plans: they will unfailingly prove blessed and profitable for us. When there can be on our part only this mere blind submission to his good pleasure, we should be content with this, since in it lies all perfection and true love of God.

The use of ordeals

Do you not know that utter dying to self, to live only in God and for God, can only take place by degrees, through a persistent fidelity in making the sacrifice of the intelligence, of the will, of all the passions and caprices, of our feelings and affections; finally and above all, the sacrifice that comes in a complete submission in all trials, in unceasing interior vicissitudes, and in states, sometimes painful indeed, through which God makes us pass in order to change us completely into him?

Do you not know that the state of pure faith excludes all things that can be perceived by the senses? In that state we go forward stripped of everything, and find no support from any created thing; but the pure light of faith remains for ever in the highest point of the soul; and by this simple light we see not only what we must do and what we must avoid, but we learn further that, by God's grace, we live in a horror of, and flight from, evil, in love and performance of good.

Do you not know that too often the sensible presence of God tends, because of its sweetness, to satisfy self-love, and that to prevent it becoming harmful to us God deprives us of it, leaving us only the presence of pure faith which has neither sweetness, nor form, nor shape, nor any manifestation whatever?—But, you object, I do not know if I possess it.—At least you know that you are for ever yearning to possess it. That must suffice you. Live in peace, in trust, in submission, in self-abandonment and in grateful love.

Do you not know that the best state of mind for holy communion is that in which God himself works in the soul? Go to communion, then, with complete self-abandonment and in that spiritual poverty and destitution in which it pleases him to put you. In that state in which nothing created or human survives, God is to be found.

To a Mother Superior experiencing deep interior peace

This profound calm you experience, this sweet and intimate peace in which you find yourself wrapped is by no means an illusion but a true work of the Holy Spirit who speaks in the depths of your heart. Peace and love, as St John of the Cross says, come together in union; peace in a perceptible fashion and love in an imperceptible but very real manner.

I am not surprised that when God deigns to accord you these precious gifts, you are not then aware of your ordinary infirmities. Your soul's interior unction is reflected in the body and expels its woes. I know people who have never found a more certain cure for their ills than this delightful recollection in God when he is pleased to grant us it; for, as you truly say, it is not from us that it comes. To be simply steadfast in the presence of God, abandoning yourself wholly to his love and to the mercy of divine Providence, is yet another indication the Holy Spirit puts into the soul. You have nothing to do except to remain simply and humbly in the hands of God, clinging to him and surrendering to his love, that of you, in you, and with you, he may do all he deems good.

Yet never stop short at that blessed peace as though it were your objective; go still farther on, for ever inclining your heart to him who gave you that peace, and emphasizing it only so far as it makes still closer your union with God who is your centre, your life and your all. You have done well to omit, as far as I am concerned, all the compliments and good wishes usual at the beginning of the year. God beholds them in your heart where they act as a personal prayer for me, even as my desires on your behalf are a prayer in God's eyes. Our desires, says St Augustine, are to God what our words and speeches are to man. He hears them, and we can hope that he will grant them.

The acceptance of weakness in suffering

To suffer in sweetness and in peace and without offering any resistance is to suffer in the right way, even though you do not then make any vigorous acts of acceptance. The submissive heart offers these, without taking thought, in the humility and simplicity of its passive acquiescence. Know further, dear Sister, that you are to thank God, as though for a grace, for what you suffer meanly and weakly, that is to say, without much courage. At such times you feel overcome by your ills, upon the verge of giving way to them, inclined to grumble about them and to yield to the rebelliousness of your human nature. Indeed, this is true grace and a great grace at that, since to suffer this is to suffer with humility and with lowliness of spirit.

If, instead, you feel a measure of courage, a measure of strength and conscious resignation, your heart is puffed up by these, and you become, yourself unaware, full of trust in yourself, interiorly proud and presumptuous. In such a state as yours, however, we draw near to God, altogether weak, humiliated and disconcerted at having suffered so feebly. This truth is sure and comforting, essentially interior, and little known.

Remember it on all those occasions upon which, feeling more keenly the weight of your tribulations and sufferings, you feel your weakness also, looking always inward in peace and simplicity to all that God wills, for this is the most satisfying way of suffering. It is what Fénelon describes as becoming little in our own eyes and allowing ourselves to be humbled by a perception of our weakness in suffering. Were this truth well known to all people of goodwill, what peace and tranquillity they would suffer, knowing neither restlessness nor any reflection of self-love on their own weakness and the lack of conscious courage with which they suffer! You must apply this rule in every painful ordeal.

Domestic trials

I admit, dear Sister, there is nothing more difficult than to maintain perfect equanimity and unswerving patience in the midst of domestic vexations and in our contact with people of a different disposition living with us. The continuity of these annoyances makes us, in a measure, powerless at times to preserve our self-control.

Yet if at one moment we fall, we rise the next. The fall is a weakness, the rising again a virtue. If we avoid a fall, we resume our serenity, knowing no vexation. Slowly God gives all things to those who can wait for them patiently. But your own desires are impetuous and you seek to be perfect all at once. We must try by degrees to modulate the turbulence and agitation of those desires that battle in our heart and threaten to break it. Now, if we are unable wholly to prevent them clashing, let us at least try to endure the affliction gently and humbly, and not set out to aggravate it by tormenting ourselves for being tormented.

The difficulties created for you and injustices done to you by people are, I admit, thoroughly disagreeable. I felt indignant at their mere recital. Yet what remedy is there for this except that of which we have already made use to cure our other ills—we must lift up our eyes to heaven saying: 'Lord, you ordain it, you have permitted it to be so; I adore and submit myself. Your blessed will be done!'

Did I know a better remedy, I would tell you of it. Yet as I am convinced that this is the most efficacious of all, you will not expect me to look for others. I admit that on such occasions it is almost impossible not to let a few signs of impatience, rebelliousness and vexation escape you, at least interiorly. Yet you must always come back to God and your better self as soon as may be, beseeching God urgently for the necessary patience.

Daily vexations

I feel keenly, dear Sister, the painfulness of the ordeal to which God submits you, and the anguish your heart must feel at the wounds you receive daily. It is true, I agree, you would need to be a saint to let such things pass and feel no kind of resentment. But if you cannot yet reach perfection in such pin-pricking vexations, endeavour at least first to banish as far as may be every thought, reflection and remark that may embitter your heart.

Second, when you cannot rid yourself of them, repeat interiorly in your most intimate soul: 'O God, you have allowed this to be; may your adorable desires and decrees be accomplished in all things: I make you a sacrifice of the difficulty and all its consequences; it shall take whatever form it pleases you: you are the Master; may you be blessed for all things and in all things; may your will be done.'

Then add further: 'For love of you, with all my heart I pardon the person who is the cause of my suffering; and, to show the sincerity of my feelings toward her, I beseech you to grant her every kind of grace, blessing and happiness.'

When your heart cries out against this, say: 'O God, you see my wretchedness; at least I long to have all these feelings, and I implore you for your grace.'

Once you have done this, think no more of it; if unworthy sentiments continue to torment you, resign yourself to endure that torment and so comply with the divine will that allows it, contenting yourself with renewing your offering in the depth of your soul. This is a noble means of sharing in the chalice of our good master, Jesus Christ.

On the loss of a spiritual director

You consider yourself much to be pitied, dear Sister, because God has deprived you of the help that he has afforded you until now. You are indeed to be pitied, but solely because of your failure to resign yourself to the plans of Providence.

Is it not deplorable that a soul whom God has chosen, whom he has admitted to his service and heaped with his graces, cannot content itself with him, but yearns earnestly for small exterior aids? Such aids are good when God gives them; but, when he withholds them, how much better is it to rely on him alone!

What joy that soul, who loves him truly, experiences in saying to him over and over again: 'O God, you are my all, I have only you, O Lord, but you suffice me, nor do I ask anything more except you.' The all-powerful hand of God then comes to take the place of the poor weak reed upon which it leaned. Assured of this, how can it consider itself forsaken and unfortunate?

You tell me that in your lonely state you can conceive of nothing that will not involve you in difficulty and affliction. How great is that grace of God which must have developed, or which of necessity will develop, in your complete detachment from all created things! Surely it is to his most cherished souls that God gives such a grace?

O daughter of little faith, yet a daughter well-beloved of God, complain in future if you dare! God alone, you go on to say, can know what I suffer. If only you do not talk so much about it, I shall congratulate you with all my heart: so used the blessed Mother Teresa to say during her great interior trials.

The fruit of patient endurance

I already see plainly, dear Sister, the rich harvest reaped in your soul by the ordeal through which God has made you pass. Although it has brought down violent storms upon you interiorly I cannot doubt but that it has helped your spiritual progress very greatly. Through it you have learnt to be crucified interiorly, to find all things repugnant, to make God constant and painful sacrifices, to discipline yourself in many things, to acquire patience, to become submissive, and to abandon yourself to God.

Yet how, you ask, can all this have come about? It has been accomplished in the highest part of your soul and often without your knowledge, by your endurance of innumerable troubles, setbacks and dislikes, even though you have been unaware of your submission, which you often practise without realizing it.

There have been times when you have been convinced that you lacked it, and that you scarcely so much as desired it. Yet then—even then—it was there in the depths of your soul. Oh, how marvellous God is in his works!

Had you known, as I, the secrets of your soul you would, it may be, have spoilt everything by hidden reversions to self and vain complacency in yourself. Let us allow God to do the work; for it is only in our ignorance, our darkness and our blindness that he can work, as he wishes, without our spoiling his work.

Even our humiliations when we believe that all goes badly and all is lost make this manifest. For you the fact that I perceive your progress clearly must be enough to make you sure of it, responsive to it, and encouraged by it.

The continuation of the same

How I would that in all things you had more trust in God, more self-abandonment to his wise and divine Providence that controls even the slightest happenings in this life! In every case he turns them to the advantage of those who put their full trust in his Providence, and who unreservedly abandon themselves to his paternal care. O God, how such trust and such utter self-surrender bring interior peace, and bring release from an infinite multiplicity of cares that are so disturbing and vexatious!

Yet as we cannot reach this state all at once, but only by slow degrees and by almost imperceptible advances, we must yearn for it ceaselessly, beseech God for it, and perform spiritual acts to secure it. We shall not lack opportunities: let us grasp them and make it our endeavour at all times to say: 'Yes, O God, you order it, you permit it thus; therefore, I too desire it out of love of you; aid and strengthen my weakness.'

All this must be said and done gently, effortlessly, in the higher part of the soul, and despite interior rebelliousness and repugnance, which we must ignore, apart from enduring them patiently and making offerings of them to God. When we fail, let us act as it is our duty to act after every one of our faults, attempting by interior humility to regain what we have lost.

Yet let this humility be gentle and tranquil without vexation or anger against ourselves any more than we feel them toward our neighbour. I mean without voluntary anger or vexation; for the initial and unintentional impulses do not depend upon ourselves; while providing that we give no consent to them, they will enable us the more meritoriously to exercise patience, gentleness and humility.

Some personal reflections

God allows my sick relative to remain still in the same state, that this may test and convert the whole family. If they profit by it, as I have every reason to hope they will, from the bottom of my heart I shall bless God for this happy mischance as of more worth than all the wealth in the world.

I have just lost the best and closest of my surviving friends—the man I most esteemed, and upon whom I most rely. God wished it so, his blessed will be done. *Fiat!* I commend him to your prayers.

God be blessed for all things and in all things! and particularly in those things of which he can make such use to sanctify his elect, each helping each! On this subject the holy Archbishop of Cambrai [Fénelon] has remarked notably: 'God often makes use of one diamond to polish another.' How greatly this thought serves to comfort us and to prevent us being shocked by the petty persecutions in which honest men reciprocally indulge.

God can easily compensate us for everything, and he does thus compensate us, when we desire nothing but him and when in him we put all our expectations. To lead us slowly and by a blessed compulsion to that good and desirable state of soul, he often takes from us all human aids and all human comfort, even as he gives a bitter taste to worldly pleasures to disgust and detach from those pleasures the worldly souls he seeks to save.

Blessed bitterness! Blessed deprivations! So should we regard them when we appreciate that they come from God's goodness rather than from his justice.

The phantoms of the mind

Could you not check both your fears and your tears, since you have so often discovered that in all that keenly affects your heart you have been liable to indulge in delusions, and to imagine non-existent terrors?

If you find it impossible to prevent these deplorable vagaries of your imagination, seek at least to profit by them in making them a subject for interior sacrifices and an opportunity for manifesting complete self-abandonment to every decree of divine Providence, whatever it be.

I agree with you: I, too, have never desired—still less have I implored—either difficulties or consolations. Those sent by Providence suffice and we have no need to desire them or secure them ourselves. Our need is to expect and to prepare for them. In this way we shall have more strength and courage with which to encounter and endure them, as we must when God sends them.

This is one of my most cherished practices, which avails me both in this life and the next. I make offering to God in advance of every sacrifice, the idea of which has entered my mind without my seeking it.

When, on the other hand, he sends us consolations, whether spiritual or temporal, we must accept them with simplicity, gratitude and thanksgiving, but without over-eagerness or excessive delight; for all joy that is not joy in God can only tend to inflame self-love.

Dependence on God alone

Interior tribulations are, as you say, the most torturing. Equally they are the most meritorious and the most purifying; while once these purifications and interior detachments are effected, life is all the sweeter because of them. It is then the easier to achieve full self-abandonment, and filial trust in God alone through Jesus Christ.

The reflections made by you upon this subject are in truth just and reasonable, though all too humanly inspired. Our need is in every case to get back from them to self-abandonment and to hope placed solely in divine Providence.

Depend then solely upon God who is for ever unchanging, who knows our needs better than we do and who supplies them unfailingly like the good Father he is. Yet he has often to deal with children so blind that they know not what they ask. In the very prayers that seem to them the most righteous and most reasonable they find delusion in that they seek to foresee a future that belongs to God alone.

When he has deprived us of what appears to us to be needful, he has the knowledge and the ability to make up for it imperceptibly by numerous secret means unknown to ourselves. So true is this that these mere shrinkings and afflictions of our hearts, when endured in patience and interior silence, advance a soul more than contact with, and blessed instruction from, the most skilful director alive.

I have had innumerable experiences of this. This then at present is your way and the one thing God asks of you: submission, self-abandonment, trust, sacrifice and silence, all to the best of your ability, but without too much violence in your efforts.

God makes everything to serve his ends

Be guided by me, dear Sister, and let us lull all our fears and entrust ourselves in all things to divine Providence with its secret and infallible means of compelling everything to serve its ends.

Whatever men can say or do, they do nothing apart from what God wishes or permits, and apart from what serves to fulfil his merciful plans. He is as mighty in achieving his ends by the most seemingly paradoxical means as he is in sustaining his servants in the midst of fiery furnaces or enabling them to walk upon the sea. We are the more conscious of Providence's paternal protection, the more filial the self-abandonment with which we put our trust in God.

I have had an experience of this very recently. Therefore with more fervour than ever I have prayed God that he shall never grant my always blind and often pernicious desires, but shall fulfil his own—just, holy, adorable and infinitely blessed as they are.

Would that you knew what joy it is to find all your peace and contentment in the mere fulfilment of the wishes of a God as good as he is mighty! Then you would long for nothing beside.

At no time consider a difficulty, whatever it be, as a sign of God's estrangement; for difficulties and tribulations, whether exterior or interior, are on the contrary the results of his goodness and of the visitations of his love.

The fear of temptation

It is an illusion to have too great a fear of spiritual conflict under the pitiable pretext that by avoiding a struggle you will avoid the danger of committing faults. Blush for your cowardice. When you find yourself face to face with contradiction or humiliation, tell yourself that the moment has come to prove to God the sincerity of your love. Trust yourself to his goodness and to the power of his grace: such trust will assure you victory.

Even when you chance to fall into this fault or that, the harm done is negligible compared with the gain you will make, whether by the efforts in the fight, or by the merit secured in the victory, or even by the humiliation caused by your minor reverses.

Now if your temptations are purely interior, and if it is through your thoughts and your feelings that you fear to be led astray, rid yourself likewise of this fear. Do not so much as directly struggle with these interior impulses; let them die down; struggle against them indirectly by means of recollection and the thought of God.

This distrust which leads you to flee temptation ordained by God calls down upon you others, still more dangerous, of which you are unaware. Let your eyes, then, be opened; recognize that all these thoughts that discourage, trouble and weaken you can come only from the devil.

I adjure you not to allow yourself to be caught in this snare, nor to let yourself look on this rebellion of your human passions as a sign of God's estrangement. No, dear daughter; it is, on the other hand, a greater grace than you imagine. By making you to perceive your weakness, it leads you to expect nothing save from God, and to rely on no one save him. God alone must suffice the soul who knows him.

The good fruits of temptation

It could almost be said, dear Sister, that you have never pondered the numerous texts in the sacred Scriptures by which the Holy Spirit gives us to understand the necessity of temptations and the valuable results they produce in souls who never allow themselves to despond.

Do you not know that they have been compared with the furnace in which clay receives its hardness and gold its gleam? Or that they are presented as a cause for rejoicing, a sign of God's regard, a lesson indispensable if knowledge of God is to be acquired?

Did you remember these comforting truths, how could you allow yourself to be overcome by melancholy? I declare to you in our Lord's name that you have no cause to fear. Do you but wish it, you can unite yourself as much as, and more than, you did in your moments of greatest fervour.

To this end you have one thing to do: endure your soul's painful state in peace and silence, with unswerving patience and utter resignation, even as you would endure a fever or other physical sickness.

From time to time you need to tell yourself what you would tell someone sick when you exhort her to bear with her sickness in patience. You would put it to her that in giving way to impatience or complaining she would merely succeed in aggravating or protracting her illness. So you must put it to yourself.

Self-love the cause of excessive fear

You fear, you say, lest your past infidelities should prevent God's operation in your soul. No, dear Sister, it is not your past infidelities, any more than your present wretchedness, helplessness and darkness, that should excite your fears. It is your lack of submission, your voluntary vexation in times of spiritual poverty, darkness and helplessness, that alone can obstruct the divine operations. Poverty, darkness and helplessness, provided they are unaccompanied by such fears, can, on the contrary, only facilitate the divine action. You have, then, nothing to fear save your fears themselves.

Now, if you wish to know what you are to do during these interior upheavals, I am going to tell you: you must remain in peaceful expectancy, silent submission and complete self-abandonment to the divine will, just as you take shelter and wait for a storm to pass, leaving God to calm the raging elements. Interior storms, tranquilly endured, effect the greatest good in the soul.

Your excessive fears upon the subject of past confessions are one more result of self-love, which wishes to be reassured in everything. God, on the other hand, wishes us to be deprived of that complete certainty. You are then, generously to make sacrifice of this certainty to the sovereign Master.

Despite these mistakes, due to your inexperience, by God's grace I find in your soul—and I rejoice at it—the two conditions essential to the divine operation: a steadfast resolution to belong unreservedly to God and a firm and constant determination to avoid the slightest deliberate faults. Persevere in that frame of mind, taking more precautions than you have done hitherto against the promptings of self-love. So shall you see the kingdom of God established within you.

The last stage to perfect union

You are experiencing a dearth of grace and strength, only because at the moment God wishes no more of you. But at no time do you have a dearth of blessed desires, since you feel so much grief at your inability to give effect to them. Remain, then, in peace in your great spiritual poverty, for it is a true treasure when we know how to accept it out of love for God.

I perceive clearly that you have never understood the true poverty and nakedness of spirit by which God succeeds in detaching us from ourselves and from our own works, the more thoroughly to purify and simplify us. This complete despoliation, which leaves us only acts of pure faith and pure love, is the last stage to perfect union. It is a true death to self, a most secret, torturing and hardly endurable death; yet a death soon rewarded with a resurrection, after which we love only for God and in God, through Jesus Christ and with Jesus Christ.

Judge your blindness from this: you are grieved by what is the surest guarantee of your spiritual advancement. After a soul has climbed the first rungs of the ladder of perfection it can make little progress except by ways of despoliation and spiritual darkness, and the way of self-obliteration and death to all created things including the spiritual.

It is only in such a state that it is able to unite itself perfectly with God, in whom is nothing we can either feel, know or experience.

Foolish fears and fancies

You are well aware that in themselves your fears are but futile fancies. Now, if it pleases God that you shall be unable to rid yourself of them completely, you have nothing to do but to drop them from you as a stone drops into water. Take no further notice of flies that come and go, buzzing in your ear. Ignore them and cultivate patience.

It is indeed surprising after all you have said and read, that you should revert once again to the interior changes and vicissitudes that you experience. This is rather as if you believed yourself obliged to note every atmospheric variation, and had to let me know that a rainy period followed a few fine days, or that a wild winter had succeeded a beautiful autumn. Such is God's established order; such are the vicissitudes of life in which all things change.

Instead of all these violent and strenuous acts that you believe yourself obliged to make, it would be far better at such times to dwell, as I have said, in the presence of God, in an interior silence of respect and humility, of submission and self-abandonment. Self-love, however, yearns always for conscious delight, That, nevertheless, cannot be, and God does not wish it. Let us then renounce it with a good grace.

It crosses your mind, I know, that you are deceiving everybody. It must be enough for you to know that you do not wish to mislead them. If it crossed your mind to kill yourself or to hurl yourself from a great height you would at once exclaim: 'I am perfectly aware that I do not want to do this—away with such follies!'

They are but so many more buzzing flies. Let us put up with them patiently. When they have flown away others will come, and these, too, we must suffer likewise in patience and resignation.

True contrition is grounded in faith

You ask the impossible, dear Sister; you seek to perceive what is imperceptible, and to give yourself assurances that we can never be given in this life. True contrition, that remits sin, is by its very nature wholly spiritual, and, it follows, independent of the senses.

It is true that, with some people on some occasions, it becomes very sensible indeed. At such times it is truly comforting to self-love, but it is not for this reason either more efficacious or more meritorious. Such sensibility in no way depends upon ourselves: therefore it is certainly not essential for the securing of the remission of our sins. A great number of souls most devoted to God scarcely ever experience this feeling, and the fears arising in these people from this deprivation are the best proof that they are not themselves responsible for it. What I have just said on the subject of contrition in general I now say in particular of the divine origin of this sorrow, which is normally least realized. You must beseech God for it, and wait for him by his grace to fill your heart with it. After this, to insist in being perturbed would be to fall into one of the devil's snares.

Nothing must so little astonish us as to find ourselves sometimes hard of heart and insensible of everything after having been stirred and deeply moved. These are inevitable vicissitudes, interiorly. May your will be done! The full remedy lies in these words. It is certain that God at all times gives to the souls that fear him the support they need. That support is not always the most obvious or the most agreeable, or the most desired, but it is the most necessary and the most enduring. Ordinarily this is the more true the less obvious that support is, and the more mortifying to self-love; for what aids us most potently to live in God is what best enables us to die to self.

The laying aside of fears

Your fears, dear Sister, have no reasonable foundation, and you must cast them from you as dangerous temptations. When in this life we make a general confession in good faith, every reflection and anxiety that come immediately after it are so many futile scruples of which the devil makes use to trouble the peace of our soul, that he may waste our time and weaken and diminish our trust in God.

Let us not stupidly deliver ourselves into this snare; let us leave all the past to God's infinite mercy, all the future to his paternal Providence, and think only of profiting by the present. A mere *fiat* at all times, and in and for all things, expressed first in repeated acts of faith and developed gradually into a set attitude of mind, constitutes in full that perfection which either through ignorance or illusion we go so far to seek outside our own spiritual state.

In conclusion, do you imagine that you shock me by speaking of your wretchedness? As a result of seeing in ourselves only poverty and misery, we learn not to be astonished at these in others. To regard them in peace and humility, making ourselves little in God's sight by demanding his grace of him, and strong with his help to decrease our faults and to subdue self out of love for him, is in a measure no longer to possess these faults.

As Fénelon, drawing on St Augustine, reminds us, we have to be reduced to the state in which we can present to God only our wretchedness and his great mercy as our one claim through the merits of Jesus Christ. Ponder these noble words at length; in them you find peace of soul, self-abandonment, trust and the great assurance in uncertainty itself.

On falling again and again

The account you have given me of your misfortunes and, in particular, of your faults and interior rebelliousness, has left me most sympathetic. Yet when it comes to a cure, I have no other than that which I have pointed out to you: each time you have new evidence of your wretchedness, humiliate yourself, make offering of it all to God, and cultivate patience.

If you once more relapse, do not be vexed and perturbed the second time as you were the first, but still more deeply humiliate yourself and, above all, do not fail to make offering to God of the interior grief and confusion caused by this rebelliousness and those faults arising from your weakness.

If you be guilty of fresh faults, with the same confidence come again to God and endure as patiently as possible the further remorse of conscience and rebellious inner grief. And let this be your invariable practice.

Be sure that as long as you do this, and as long as you struggle with yourself in this way, scarcely anything will be lost; in fact much will be gained as the result of the involuntary interior rebelliousness which you suffer.

Whatever the fault that escapes you, provided that you consistently seek to recollect yourself and to come back to God, in the way that has just been explained to you, it is impossible for you to fail to make good progress. If once and for all you learn to humiliate yourself sincerely for your slightest faults by sweetly and peacefully allowing your trust in God to pick you up again straightaway, you will provide yourself with a good and assured remedy for the past, and a potent and efficacious safeguard for the future.

A difficult personal relationship

There is no need for me to go into much detail upon the subject of that lively and keenly felt grief of which you tell me. I understand all the varied and afflicting reflections that make a treadmill of your head, and all the anguish of your heart.

Yet in these, dear daughter, you have an excellent prayer that will sanctify you far more than spiritual ecstasies, if you but know how to profit by them. How can you do so? In this way:

Pray constantly for the person who has caused you this vexation.

Keep completely silent, speaking of it to no one in order to lighten your grief.

Do not voluntarily think of it, but direct your mind to blessed and useful thoughts.

Keep watch over your heart, lest it surrender itself even in the slightest to bitterness, vexation, murmuring and voluntary rebelliousness.

Cost what it may, seek to speak well of this person, to be favourably disposed toward her, and to behave toward her as though nothing had happened.

I realize, however, that it would be difficult for you to have the trust in her you once had—at least, unless you were the saint you have not yet become. But, at least, never fail to help her at every opportunity, and to wish her every possible good.

In times of deep suffering

Be of good courage, dear Sister, and do not imagine yourself to be estranged from God. On the contrary, you have never been nearer to him.

Remember our Lord's agony in the Garden of Olives, and you will realize that bitterness of heart and anguish of spirit are not incompatible with perfect submission. These are the outcries of suffering nature, and signs of the difficulty of the sacrifice.

Do nothing, then, against God's decree, nor utter one word of complaint or lamentation. In this lies that perfect submission which is born of love, and of the purest love at that. At such junctures, would that you could do nothing and say nothing, but dwell in a humble silence of respect, faith, adoration, submission, self-abandonment and sacrifice: then you have discovered the great secret of sanctifying all your sufferings, and even of turning them into great sweetness.

You must strive for this state and seek to make it habitual, but when you have failed in it, you must be careful not to fall into grief or discouragement, returning rather to that great silence in peaceful and tranquil humility.

For the rest, rely with an unswerving trust on the help of grace, which can never be denied you.

Giving the devil his chance

At no time take heed of those diabolical thoughts that would lead you to say: 'I am for ever the same, for ever as lacking in recollection, as prone to distraction, as impatient and imperfect.'

All this vexes you interiorly, burdens your heart, and leads you to a melancholy distrust and discouragement, and so plays the devil's game. By this feigned humility and this regret for your faults he rejoices to deprive us of the strength we need to shun, and atone for, those faults in the future.

Bitterness spoils everything; sweetness, on the other hand, can cure everything. Be, then, greatly tolerant of yourself, gently return to God; gently repent, showing neither exterior nor interior anxiety, but cultivating peacefulness of spirit.

This one practice, carried out with thoroughness, will, as time goes on, secure your interior calm, and will enable you to advance farther on God's way than all your agitation can ever do. When we feel a measure of gentleness and of peace in our hearts, we take pleasure in returning to that way, and willingly carrying out that practice, doing so consistently, easily and almost without taking thought.

Be guided by me, dear Sister; put all your trust in none but God, through Jesus Christ; in all things and for all things, abandon yourself more and more utterly to him, and you shall know by experience that he will always come to your help in times of need.

He will constitute himself your Master, your guide, your support, your protector, your invincible strength. Then you will no longer lack anything; for who has God has all.

Be gentle with yourself

The character of the person you sketch for me is, I admit, very good; yet while you praise God for the gifts he has granted her, you must not despise the lot he has accorded yourself.

Your need, in fact, is that you should never know bitterness of heart in any connection whatever, but should always be gentle with yourself. For is it not true that this is how you behave toward your neighbour? You would not for ever be making bitter attacks upon his character, but would try gently to induce him to reform it.

Behave in this way in regard to yourself; then, should this spirit of gentleness, by slow degrees, be instilled into your heart, you will speedily and without so much difficulty make progress in the interior life. Yet if the heart be constantly filled with vexation and bitterness, we achieve little and that at an infinite cost.

I emphasize the point strongly because it is one of your essential needs; while, were I in your place, I should in all things study to acquire a great interior and exterior gentleness, as if there were no other virtue open to me to practise; for in your case gentleness must needs bring you to all the rest.

I appeal to your own experience; when for some time you have worked placidly, not indulging in that impetuousness and over-eagerness which banishes gentleness instead of ensuring its acquirement, you yourself will recognize that by this means our gains are greater in that we tire ourselves less.

Various difficulties

No longer give way to the grief that arises from the difficulty you experience in concentrating your attention. Remember that the mere desire, if habitual, of recollection can serve in recollection's stead, and that we have only to be unfailing in our desire to think of God, please God, and obey God, in order to think of, please, and obey him indeed.

The greater your wish to learn to pray, you say, the less is your ability for prayer. That might well be because your wish is not accompanied by a sufficiently complete submission and purity of intention. Always go to prayer with the one desire to please God, and not to draw conscious delight from it. Go to it in a spirit of sacrifice and to get out of it all that should be pleasing to God. Realize, moreover, that recollection is like those things that escape our minds when we are over-anxious to remember them, but that return to us when we treat them with a certain passive indifference: this is the teaching of St Francis de Sales.

Never lose sight of that great precept that asserts that great spiritual poverty, known, felt and loved out of love of the abjection it brings, is one of the greatest treasures that a soul can possess in this world, since knowledge of it keeps the soul in deep humility. To believe, on the other hand, that you are lost because you make no discovery in yourself of clearly perceived faith and charity, and to be thereupon vexed, disquieted, or discouraged, is a dangerous illusion of self-love, that for ever longs to see all things clearly, and in all things to have reason for self-complacency. When we experience this temptation we must say to ourselves: I have been, I am and I shall be all that shall please God; yet, intellectually and in the apex of my soul, I want to belong to him and serve him, whatever may befall me in this world or the next.

Hope in God alone

The absence of hope grieves you more than any other trial. Let me, with God's grace, try to cure you of this ill.

You want, dear Sister, to find a little help in yourself and your good works? That is precisely what God does not wish; that is what he cannot tolerate in souls that aspire to perfection.

What! rely upon self, count upon your good works—what a wretched survival of self-love, pride and perversity! It is to rid chosen souls of these that God makes them pass through a desolating state of poverty, wretchedness and spiritual nakedness. He wishes slowly to destroy all the trust and reliance they have in themselves, to deprive them of all their resources, so that he may be their sole support, their sole trust, their one hope, their one resource!

How accursed is that hope which unreflectingly you thus seek in yourself! How glad I am that God destroys, confounds and obliterates that cursed hope by means of this state of poverty and wretchedness! When all trust, all hope, all earthly and created aids have been taken from us, we shall have no more aid, we shall have no more trust, we shall have no more hope save in God alone.

This is the right hope, the right trust known to the saints, a hope and a trust based solely upon the mercy of God and the merits of Jesus Christ. But you will have this hope only after God has destroyed in you the last clinging roots of your trust in self. This may come to pass only if God keeps you for a while yet in entire spiritual poverty.

Think only on God's mercy

Yet, you will say, of what use to us are good works if they are not to inspire us with trust? Their use is to secure us the grace of a still more complete distrust in ourselves and a still greater trust in none but God. This is the sole use the saints made of them.

To what, indeed, do our works amount? They are so spoilt and so corrupted by our self-love that if God judged us rigorously, we should deserve more punishment than reward. Give no further thought, then, to your good works as a means of enjoying tranquillity at death: merely fix your eyes on the mercy of God, the merits of Jesus Christ, the intercession of the saints and the prayers of righteous souls.

Turn then away from everything—everything that might give you occasion to rely upon yourself, or even in the smallest measure to place your trust in your own good works.

The remarks you make to others—or rather the remarks God gives you to make—in the time of your greatest spiritual aridity do not surprise me at all. It is God's usual attitude, determined by the fact that his wish is to console others, the while he keeps you in desolation and self-abandonment. At such times you speak what God gives you to speak, leaving you dead to all feeling in yourself but alive in the feeling you have for others. I see no manner of hypocrisy in this.

Let it all be in God's time

To avoid dissipation in the tasks that your obedience sets you to do, you need but to go about them placidly, showing neither anxiety nor over-eagerness; while to perform them in this way you have, says St Francis de Sales, but to do them wholly out of love for God and obedience to God.

For, the same saint adds, since this love is gentle and persuasive, all that it inspires us to do has the same nature. But when self-love intervenes with its desires for success and self-satisfaction—that desire is its constant companion—first it imports an element of human activity and eagerness, and then anxiety and grief.

Be that as it may, you will tell me, I am quite convinced that these tasks hinder advancement. When, dear Sister, we love only the love of God, we wish to advance only as much as God wishes; we abandon ourselves to his divine Providence for our spiritual progress, even as good men in the world abandon themselves to that Providence for the success of their temporal concerns.

Yet the great evil is that our self-love intrudes everywhere, interfering and spoiling everything, once more to quote St Francis de Sales. It is self-love that converts even the desire to advance spiritually into a subject of self-satisfaction and a cause of grief, and, consequently, into a stumbling-block to our advancement.

Perseverance in darkness

You see nothing in your present state. In the midst of this obscure night, go forward, then, by the light of blind obedience. It is a safe guide that has never yet led anyone astray, and whose guidance is more sure and more speedy than that of even the most perfect acts of self-abandonment.

Such acts are indeed excellent, though it is possible that you may sometimes find yourself unable to perform them. On such occasions you will be able to put yourself in a still more perfect state, which consists in dwelling in the interior silence of respect, adoration and submission, of which I have written so much.

Such silence tells God more than all your formal acts. Moreover, it knows no return to self-complacency and is without consolations perceptible to the senses. Here you have the true mystical death, which must necessarily precede the supernatural life of grace.

Unless God perceives in you this second death—death to spiritual consolation—you will not attain to this wholly spiritual and interior life for which you long so fervently.

Spiritual consolations are in fact so sweet that, were not God to detach us from them by the violence of spiritual ordeals, we should become even more attached to them than to any worldly pleasure, and this would be a supreme stumbling-block to perfect union.

Take courage in realizing that those things that today constitute your sorrow and your martyrdom will in a day to come be your greatest delight. When will that blessed time be? God alone knows; it will be when it pleases him.

A hurtful and dangerous temptation

The terrors caused by your old faults are the most dangerous and hurtful of your temptations. Hence I order you to reject all such advances of the devil, as we reject the temptations of blasphemy and impurity. Think only of the present and shut yourself up in the will of God, leaving all else to his Providence and mercy.

Your stupidity and insensibility are emphatically not punishments for some hidden sin, as the devil would have you think, so that your interior peace may be troubled. They are pure graces, which have indeed a bitter taste, and yet have had good effects already, and in the future will have still more. Who says so? I—on God's behalf—assure you that it is so.

I should have been sorry indeed to have had the foolish satisfaction of hearing your general confession. For that would have delivered you into the devil's snare. What are you, then, to do to be rid of these fears? You are to obey simply and blindly him who speaks to you on behalf of the Master who has deputed him for the part, and voluntarily, give no further thought to it.

Your sole interior practice must be to continue to dwell, as you now do, in the hands of God, much as a rough stone that is shaped, fashioned and polished by the sharp blows from hammer and chisel. In patience wait for the sovereign architect to indicate that niche in his edifice in which he shall choose to set you, once he has shaped and fashioned you with his hand.

Trials to be suffered until relieved

The difficulties in your soul's lower part when your griefs are most poignant can never destroy your peace of spirit, as long as your submission to God is complete. This is known as possessing the solid and undoubted peace of God.

As for painful thoughts, extravagances to the imagination and other temptations, you must allow them to drop from you so far as you are able, as a stone sinks into water.

When you cannot succeed in this, as often happens in time of ordeal, you must allow yourself to be crucified as it shall please God, and endure your sickness of soul as you would that of the body, in patience, submission, trust and utter self-abandonment, and desiring only the will of God, in union with Jesus Christ.

The deep-seated desire for recollection is in itself true recollection, though no delight accompany it. If it is less consoling than sensible recollection, it is only the more unselfish for that, and, it follows, the more meritorious. In such a state we call nothing ours, since it seems to us that we possess nothing.

As long as your present ordeal lasts, you must make your renunciation consist chiefly in accepting this ordeal with complete submission. Much still remains for you to do if you are to attain to this perfect self-abandonment. Realize that your internal upheaval will cease only when you have surrendered yourself unreservedly, endlessly and limitlessly to God's every wish.

May God be blessed for all things and in all things! Amen.

The painful awareness of our nothingness

The vivid awareness you feel of your nothingness in God's sight is one of the most salutary operations of the grace of the Holy Spirit. I know how thoroughly painful this operation can be; the poor soul appears to be on the brink of utter obliteration, whereas it is only nearer to true life.

Indeed the deeper we are plunged into our nothingness, the nearer we are to truth, since our very essence is of that nothingness from which we have been drawn out by the Lord's pure goodness. We ought, then, to dwell in that unbrokenly, and thus, by our voluntary self-obliteration, render continual homage to the grandeur and infinite nature of our Creator. Such sacrifice is a holocaust in which self-love is utterly consumed in the fire of divine love.

When this sorrowful, yet blessed, hour has come, we have nothing to do but imitate Jesus Christ on the cross: we must commend our soul to God, surrender ourselves still more completely to all that it pleases the sovereign Master to do with this poor creature, and remain in that agony as long as his good pleasure ordains.

Let us be of good courage, dear daughter: let us assent to everything with the blessed abasement of spirit of Jesus Christ crucified. From all this our strength must come. Let us make a habit of saying, when such anguish besets us: 'Indeed, Lord, I desire all that you desire, in Jesus Christ and through Jesus Christ!' In such company as his, how could we be afraid? In the most violent temptations a simple abasement at the feet of the Saviour-God will make all things calm: he will render you victorious; while, with his strength, he will enable your weakness to triumph over all the tempter's cunning.

A good foundation for humility

May God be blessed, Reverend Mother, for the notable graces which it has pleased him to accord you! Your chief care henceforth must be to guard these precious gifts with watchful humility.

Your experience of the peace of God during prayer comes, without a doubt, from the Holy Spirit. Take care lest, by a most ill-advised multiplication of your religious acts, you emerge from that simplicity which is the more fruitful the nearer it approaches the infinite simplicity of God. This way of knowing union with him through a complete effacement of the self is based upon the great principle that our Almighty and all-good God gives his children ... what he knows will be most fitting for them, and that the whole of perfection lies in the heart's steadfast clinging to his adorable will.

To be in no way astonished at our wretchedness is a good foundation for humility based upon self-knowledge: while to feel that wretchedness keenly and constantly, and yet to be untroubled by it, is a very great grace from which spring distrust of self and true and perfect trust in God. Your devotion to the sacred Heart of Jesus and the practices you have adopted in regard to it are true spiritual treasure that suffices to enrich both you and your dear daughters. The more you draw upon this treasure, the more there remains for you to draw, inexhaustible as it is.

A spirit of gentleness and moderation in government is a noble gift from heaven; government is the more effectual and salutary for this spirit. When we fall let us humiliate ourselves, pick ourselves up, and continue our way in peace. That way is at all times to ponder upon the true self which is God—God in whom we must plunge and lose ourselves, rather as we shall find ourselves plunged and lost in heaven, in the everlasting duration of eternity's great day. Amen! Amen!

Sources and index

There are seven 'books' of Caussade's letters and these are bound in a single volume, *Self-abandonment to Divine Providence*, translated from the French by Algar Thorold, edited by James Joyce, SJ, and published by Burns & Oates in their *Orchard Books*. This volume, which is now out of print, also contains Caussade's treatise on Abandonment and his spiritual counsels. All the selections in *The Fire of Divine Love* are taken, with very minor adjustments, from this translation. In the index on the following two pages, the numbers 23 to 122 in bold type refer to pages of this present book; the letter C stands for Counsel (C 4=Counsel 4), and from page 31 onwards the figure before the colon refers to the number of the Caussade 'book', the other figure referring to the number of the letter. Thus **49** 2:14 means that page 49 of this book is taken from letter 14 of Caussade's second 'book'.

Readers who possess *Abandonment to the Divine Providence* (which is also out of print), translated by E. J. Strickland and published by the Catholic Records Press (Exeter, 1921), will also be able to use the index to refer to the selected letters. Caussade's letters have also been published in smaller books, each of two or three 'books'. The index will also avail here.

In making these selections from Caussade's letters I have had to work to the discipline of the single page and to make each page speak for itself. This has meant taking a few liberties with the original such as an occasional adjustment in the wording of the opening sentence of a page. In some letters omissions have been made to bring the message within the allotted space. I have felt that to insert dots would impede the flow and perhaps be tedious to the reader. Care has been taken to see that Caussade's meaning remains unchanged.

Reading Page	Source		Reading Page	Source
23	C	1	51	2: 17
24	C	2	52	2: 35
25	C	2	53	2: 36
26	C	3	54	3: 1
27	C	4	55	3: 1
28	C	4	56	3: 3
29	C	5	57	3: 3
30	C	5	58	3: 3
31	1:	1	59	3: 3
32	1:	2	60	3: 3
33	1:	3	61	3: 4
34	1:	4	62	3: 4
35	1:	5	63	3: 4
36	1:	7	64	3: 4
37	1:	9	65	3: 4
38	1: 10		66	3: 4
39	2:	1	67	3: 7
40	2:	1	68	3: 10
41	2:	4	69	3: 11
42	2:	5	70	3: 13
43	2:	6	71	3: 13
44	2: 10		72	3: 15
45	2: 11		73	3: 16
46	2: 11		74	4: 1
47	2: 12		75	4: 1
48	2: 13		76	4: 1
49	2: 14		77	4: 1
50	2: 14		78	4: 3

Reading Page	Source	Reading Page	Source
79	4: 5	107	6: 13
80	4: 5	108	6: 11
81	4: 5	109	6: 19
82	4: 6	110	6: 20
83	4: 7	111	6: 21
84	4: 8	112	6: 22
85	4: 10	113	6: 22
86	4: 11	114	6: 26
87	4: 14	115	7: 1
88	4: 15	116	7: 1
89	4: 15	117	7: 1
90	4: 18	118	7: 2
91	4: 20	119	7: 2
92	5: 1	120	7: 8
93	5: 7	121	7: 9
94	5: 9	122	7: 18
95	5: 11		
96	5: 15		
97	5: 15		
98	5: 16		
99	5: 17		
100	5: 17		
101	5: 18		
102	6: 2		
103	6: 3		
104	6: 6		
105	6: 7		
106	6: 9